The European New Right
— A Shi'a Response

A Radical Critique of Alexander Dugin,
E. Michael Jones, and Alain de Benoist

Arash Najaf-Zadeh

The European New Right - A Shi'a Response

A Radical Critique of Alexander Dugin,
E. Michael Jones, and Alain de Benoist

Arash Najaf-Zadeh

Copyright © 2018 Black House Publishing Ltd

All rights reserved. No part of this book may be reproduced in any form by any electronic or mechanical means including photocopying, recording, or information storage and retrieval without permission in writing from the publisher.

ISBN-13: 978-1-912759-06-4

Black House Publishing Ltd
Kemp House
152 City Road
London
United Kingdom
EC1V 2NX

www.blackhousepublishing.com

Email: info@blackhousepublishing.com

For my beloved wife Faranak,
without whom none of my work would have been possible.

Contents

Précis	1
Preamble	11
1. *Ex Oriente Lux*	17
2. The Metaphysics of Chaos	23
3. Finitude and the Tripartite Proof	27
4. Elaborations on the Proof of Finitude	35
Apophatic Theology	35
The Criterion of Quantifiability	37
Any Possible Being must Necessarily have a Creator	39
The Singularity and Dualist Ontology	40
The Fallacy of "Pre-Eternity" and "Post-Eternity"	41
The Incarnation	43
The Incarnation through the Lens of John Hick	44
5. *al-Haqq* and the Referential Theory of Knowledge	51
6. Philosophical Ding-Dong at the Mad Hatter's Tea Party	59
7. Philosophy as the Continuance of a Pagan Farce	63
8. The "Curious Disputations" of Greek Philosophy	69
9. Alain de Benoist contra the Totalitarians	77
10. From Unipolarity to Multipolarity	81
11. From Multipolarity Back to Unipolarity	87
12. *Dasein* and the *Barzakh*	95
Tanzīh, Tashbīh, Ta'tīl	97
Symbol, Incarnation, Theophany	100
Will to Power or Will to Faith	101

Contents

13. Logos and the Light of the Eye ... 103
   - *The Lord of the Flies* ... 105
   - *Hayy eben Yaqzān* or *Intelligentia ex Nihilo* ... 109
   - "The Word" between Athens and Jerusalem ... 111
   - Pre-Ontological Chaos ... 113
   - Excursus: Children Deprived of Revelation ... 117
14. Objective Truth and Radical Postmodern Subjectivism ... 119
   - The Imam is Occulted ... 119
   - The Impossibility of a Non-Foundationalist Paradigm ... 123
   - The False Appeal of the Perennialists ... 129
   - *Extra Ecclesiam nulla Salus* and its Alternative: the Zombification of the Soul ... 131
15. Welāyat and the Principal of Tavallī and Tabarrī ... 137

Summary and Conclusion ... 149

Précis

Other than the order that liberal democracy is trying to impose on the world, and other than the political form of Shi'a Islam which came to the fore after the triumph of the Islamic Revolution of 1979, there seems to be three main alternatives on offer. The first and most important of these is Alexander Dugin's Eurasianist movement, after which we can mention Alain de Benoist and the Grecists (even though he is less well known than Alain Soral or Eric Zemmour), and traditional Catholicism. Because the dominant paradigm is ideologically bankrupt and dying (and also because its home-grown European adversaries have done a fine job in criticizing it), we have chosen to respond to its most prominent adversaries. But because Shi'a Islam is something that is not at all well-understood, we first need to mention briefly where we are coming from and how that differs from what is known as Shi'a Islam in the West.

In the academic community, there are three kinds of Shi'a Islam on offer: that which has been interpreted and presented by Henry Corbin and his teacher, Louis Massignon. This is a philosophical approach to Shi'a Islam which is deeply imbued with complex philosophical ideations and sophisticated philosophical jargon and which, moreover, ignores many of the basic tenets of the religion in favor of its philosophical-rational approach which does not reflect the faith as it is understood by the millennial tradition of its clerisy and practitioners. The Islam of the Muhyiddin Ibn 'Arabi Society and writers such as William Chittick, James Morris, and Ralph Austin suffers from the same bias. The basic assumptions of this bias which lead to Eben 'Arabī's theory of the unicity of being (*wahdat al-wujud*) and to the "transcendental wisdom" (*hekmat-e mote'ālīa*) of Molla Sadrā is refuted in this essay by the Proof of Finitude and its implications (Sections 3 and 4, respectively).

The other type of Shi'a Islam that is grist for the mill for some academics (such as Seyyed Hossein Nasr), but is also popular among non-Academics is the Perennialist version which has been promulgated by Rene Guenon, Charles Eaton, Titus Burkhardt, Frithjof Schuon, Martin Lings, and not least, by Seyyed Hosein Nasr himself. The problem with this school is that in the final analysis, it is

The European New Right - A Shia Response

ultimately subjectivist in its epistemology and pluralist in its ontology. How they can reconcile this with the categorical need of having the sacred as front and center in any religion, and the fact that the sacred is absolutely sacred and not relatively so, is beyond me. But there it is. We have dealt with the fallacy of this movement in the last three of the four subsections in chapter 14.

And finally, within academia, there is, of course, the orientalist approach, which is either agnostic and supposedly "detached" and "objective", as in the orientalism of Mohammad Ali Amīr-Moezzī; or is atheistic and hostile, as in the orientalism of the British Ministry of Intelligence agents such as Ann Lambton, formerly of that den of spies, SOAS, and her worthy successor, Bernard Lewis of Princeton; or is theistic and not-so-hostile, as in the orientalism of Montgomery Watt or Kenneth Cragg, or is theistic and hostile, as in the orientalism of the competent but ultimately misguided late Patricia Crone, for example. All of these hold positions that are supposedly unbiased, but which are radically anti-Islamic and extremely toxic to the Shi'a faithful, and are to be handled with extreme care, unless one is trained in and is equipped with the proper dogmatic and apologetic apparatus for dealing with their false assumptions, spurious arguments and false memes.

And outside the academy and within the seminary, there is the Shi'a Islam that is referred to as "British Islam" (*tashayyo'-e engelīsī*) by Ayatollah Khāmeneī, by which he is mainly referring to the Shi'a Islam of the Ayatollah Shīrāzī clan and to that of the Kho'ī Foundation, both of which are based in London and are ardent advocates of the separation of mosque and state, which would lead one to believe that they certainly have the tacit support of London, and most probably enjoy its active financial support as well. The most eloquent mouthpiece for this kind of apolitical Islam which does not suffer from the philosophical methodological error of the academics or from the pluralist ontological error of the Perennialists (but which ultimately fails at the final hurdle, which is the political), is Seyed Ammar Nakshawani (Seyyed Ammar Nakhjavānī) of the Hartford Seminary. The error of this group has not been dealt with in this essay, but has been given a full treatment in two of our other books.[1]

---

[1] See *Creedal Foundations of Walīyic Islam*, Lion of Najaf Publishers, 2017, which deals with the creedal reasons why Islam and Shi'a Islam in particular must necessarily be

Précis

And so, because Brother Alexander Dugin's familiarity with Islam has mainly been informed by Henry Corbin's perspective and by that of the Perennialists, we felt the need to include Sections 3 and 4 to establish the metaphysical perspective of the authentic Shi'a Islam which he and everyone else in the West is not heretofore familiar with – the alternative which is completely misunderstood, if understood at all, and which is usually characterized as the "fundamentalist" Islam of the "Mad Mullas" (but whose proper designation is "Walīyic Islam"). Given this massive disconnect that leads people to believe that what we have in Iran, the Besieged Shi'a Citadel, is a form of "fundamentalism", then we are happy to oblige those who have bought into this false meme by putting the "fun" back into "fundamentalism". But to continue on a serious note… because the Catholic tradition as well as Alexander Dugin's approach suffers from a methodological error which is the whole edifice of philosophy itself, we felt the need to provide a criticism of this methodological error from the Shi'a perspective, which we have done in sections 5 through 8.

Chapter 9 deals with Alain de Benoist's perspective, which is an amalgam of the pantheism of pagan Europe and the polytheism of ancient Greece, and which holds that *logos* was itself originally just another expression of *mythos* as "the image of the idea precedes and is frequently more pregnant than its discursive formulation". This type of "mythic" thinking is very alluring to the sophisticated rationalists who don't necessarily see the limitations of reason but *sense* it, yet have not seen or for whatever reason do not want to see and then enter into the door of Divine Revelation. The mentality is nicely gathered in the oh-so-sophisticated Princeton/Bollingen Mythos Series in World Mythology, which is authored by the likes of Eliade, Corbin, Malinowski, Jung, the Perennialists, etc. whose initially non-religious study of comparative religion (or of the philosophy of religion) and the detection and gathering and classification of bizarre patterns in the human psyche has become so "deep" as to take on the characteristics of a veritable religion itself. All we need now to form the next level of our infinitely regressive philosophico-religious formation of caryatids is a new Malinowski to identify it and an Eliade to catalogue it.

---

political; and *The Regency of the Magisterium*, Lion of Najaf Publishers, 2017, which deals with the political superstructure of the constitutional order of the Islamic Republic.

The European New Right - A Shia Response

From there we turn from dealing with basic assumptions and methodological errors to substantive issues; and the first of these is the issue of unipolarity and multipolarity. These two sections deal with the issue which prompted me to write this response to Brother Alexander in the first place. Alexander Dugin, being a pluralist and cultural relativist, believes that we are moving away from the unipolar moment which arose as a result of the collapse of the Soviet Union, into a multipolar world, each with its own ontic pole. Thus, Brother Dugin talks about different "humanities" (in the plural) and different ontic realities. We contend, contra this pluralist error, that humanity is and has always been singular in its essence and metaphysical reality, which is a universally applicable and trans-temporal moral one (although we have not been unitary in our actions and superficial attributes due to the latitude which we have by virtue of the limited free will which we have been given by our Maker.) The true and actual nature of the world, we argue, is unipolar in the sense that there is only one God, and He has created creation in a certain way that is in conformance with His will; and at the level of the human domain, any human being who conforms his or her will to that of God's, will thereby have lived a moral life, and anyone who does not do so will have lived a life that is less than moral. The nature and fabric of Creation are such that if we submit our will to that of God's, Who has absolute exclusivity of Providential Lordship over His creation, our decisions will naturally result in a greater spiritual proximity to the one and only Source of Perpetuity, and if we choose to live a life that is contrary to His will and contrary to Truth and Justice, then we will have distanced ourselves from that source, and will, by definition, wither away after judgement day, because it is only God who is eternal, and anything that does not abide in Him or is not sustained by His leave withers away.

Thus, the original unity of creed and purpose which obtained at the time of Adam and Eve can and should rightly be described as the original state of unipolarity, because it was in conformance and harmony with the unchanging moral and metaphysical reality that is in God and which is infused in His creation and which constitutes the warps and woofs of its very fabric. This original and *actual* "unipolar moment" was shattered when Kane murdered Able, at the dawn of human history.

Précis

The important insight which arises from our perspective is that as the various poles of the world (be it Russian Orthodoxy and the Third Rome, the emergent political Islam and of the Axis of Resistance, or the Middle Kingdom of Confucian China, or whatever else, such as a Pagan revival in Europe) – as these various poles emerge in opposition to the hegemonic ambitions of the dying zombie empire (or the Empire of Chaos, as my buddy the brilliant Postmodern Nomad Pepe Escobar has characterized it), the tendency is not going to be their ineluctable emergence as such (as assumed by Brother Alexander), but rather, their *inability* to emerge, and their repeated frustrations at their repeated attempts at doing so; and more importantly, the obviation of the phenomenon which is the attenuation and dissipation of the very cores of all these poles, (including that of the Shi'a Citadel). In other words, what is happening, in our estimation, is not a process of coagulation or crystallization and emanation and emergence of new poles against a unitary or dominant one, but a process of the dissolution and disintegration of all of the existing poles, be they that of the dominant paradigm of liberal capitalism, that of Catholicism, of Russian Orthodoxy and the Third Rome, of Sunnite Islam, and not least and certainly including that of Shi'a Islam.

This is the process which was first characterized by Jean-François Lyotard as the collapse of the *grand récit* or Great Narrative, and which is the central characteristic of the postmodern condition, and which we characterize as the central condition of the End Times. It is a process of the attenuation and dissipation and disappearance of the belief in the ontological reality of God (and hence in an objective reality to which truth and justice can be "referred" in the referential theory of truth and justice), without belief in Whom one cannot have meaning in any real sense, i.e. an objective meaning that is accessible to all of humanity, by which we can all be expected to live and by whose criteria we can therefore be judged. It is the process of the realization that there is no longer an unimpeachable authority *(hojjat)*. It is a process, in other words, of the gradual realization of the fact that *the Imam is occulted* (just as the Catholic *sede vacantists* have become Shi'a in a very real and important sense, as they see that the seat of their Pope is vacant, and that this is, in effect, in what we Shi'a call a state of occutation). I do not know this, but I imagine the Russian Old Believers must believe that they have similar stigmata on the body of their religions institution.

The European New Right - A Shia Response

Our position and contention is that we are lost without guidance from above, and because we have rejected this guidance over and over again, and killed all of the prophets and Imams, our condition is beyond repair absent the advent of that Divine Guide and absent the Second Coming of the Christ Jesus, the son of Mary (unto all of whom be God's peace). All we can do is to work to the best of our ability in the seemingly Sisyphusian task of attempting to establish God's will on Earth as it is in Heaven in the absence of divine guidance while being conscious of the impossibility of our task, and having faith that the advent of the promised savior will come before too long.

The *consciousness* of this impossibility will prevent us from falling into the error and heresy of Pelagianism; but the function of the impossibility – the impossibility of having different poles live as different "humanities" in peace with each other – an impossibility which will become more and more obviated as we spiral ever steeper into the vortex at the end of history and towards the *telos* of history or to the eschaton – the telosic *function* of this impossibility is to awaken humanity from its absurd, self-assured and arrogant humanism, and to engender in mankind that original spiritual sense of dependence on a Higher Power, and subsequent need for Guidance from Above. To awaken, in other words, the original religious consciousness and impetus in mankind, and to humble his arrogance, so that he can better conform himself to the true reality which is God, and not to those pseudo-realities and poles which we forged for ourselves as we glory in our arrogance; so that we can find salvation through God and the message that He has sent to us through His Apostles. The function of what I will call the Vortex of Impossibility is to catalyze the consciousness in man of his dependence on a higher power and to move away from the self-satisfied and false sense of security of secular humanism toward the ineluctable need for a Universal Savior, who is the only one who can restore the one and only true order, the *ordo dei*. The impossibility, in other words, acts as yet another Portal of Grace.

Chapter 12 is the opening volley in our substantive argument against Heideggerian ontological pluralism, which is based on his characterizing being as "situated human existence". Heidegger, we say, rightly situates the human being in a time-bound context, which makes it contextual and therefore relative to its and other contexts. That is good and well, as far as it goes. The difference that arises

Précis

between his cosmologies and anthropologies and those of the Quran's relate to the next question which has to do with the nature of *where exactly we are situated*. In other words, yes, we are located in time; but where, pray, is time *itself* located?! Revealed knowledge tells us that we and all time-bound reality are located *in the womb of the barzakh,* which is an intermediate realm between this, the lower world (the *donyā*), and Heaven and Hell, which have an incomparably higher ontic intensity than that which we are used to experiencing in this, the lowest world and the lowest order of being, in other words. And if we were to step back to this *Punctum Archimedis*, as revealed knowledge can and does, we would indubitably conclude that the "original essence of being" is not time, as Heidegger states, but *beyond* time. We are in the *barzakh* while we are still "in the womb" (our world), but we enter it proper upon our death, upon which event its veil is lifted, as the veil of the world is gradually lifted from an infant once he or she exits in his or her mother's womb.

The chapter continues the discussion of Heidegger's belief that "like being, truth is necessarily historical"; a belief which therefore denies "the existence of a rational order outside history". We argue that neither being nor truth are historical in their essence, as all things that are truly real obtain and exist only in God, Who, indeed, is none other than "the existence of a rational order outside history". We conclude the chapter by stating that a pluralist position such as that which Brothers Heidegger and Dugin maintain fails to produce *an objective basis for communal judgment* and is thus ultimately nihilistic as it denies the possibility of the Day of Judgement, denies the possibility of Resurrection, of Heaven and Hell, and of everlasting life in the Hereafter. Thus, in a pluralist morality, because one can only have subjective or inter-subjective meaning, morality becomes a question of choosing between a will to power or a will to faith; or a will to materialist, hedonist, narcissist nihilism or a will to brotherly communal existence in this world and eternal felicity in the Hereafter.

In the next section, Chapter 13 (Logos and the Analogy of the Light of the Eye), we talk about the true nature of logos from an Islamic perspective, and liken it to a faculty of understanding which, like the human eye, is an innate part of the human anatomy. And like the physical eye which cannot operate or see anything without there being light, the eye of the faculty of intellection (*'aql*) cannot see anything of the innate order of creation without the light of revelation shining onto it. And so, given this analogy, because the Imam is occulted, we are, in a very real sense, snow blind. In other words, we can see, but there are so many patterns out there that without divine guidance and without that divinely-sanctioned unimpeachable authority *(hojjat)*, we are no longer able properly to distinguish between right and wrong patterns of behavior. And this is especially true when it comes to the public or social domain, where the tentacles of the Westphalian order have profaned even the traditional society of the Islamic Republic of Iran and has turned it from a community (*ommaʿ*) to a "civil" society (*jāmeʿe-ye madanī*).

In this same chapter we contrast the story of Eben Tofayl's *Hayy eben Yaqzān* with that of William Golding's *Lord of the Flies*. *Hayy eben Yaqzān* is the story of a child raised by a doe on an equatorial island who grows up to discover the truth about the world and his own place in it, unaided—but also unimpeded—by society, language, or tradition. His *innate intelligence*, feeble at first, develops by degrees, until it enables him to dominate his brute companions... Thence he advances into the realm of metaphysics and proves for himself the existence of an all-powerful Creator... At the end of seven times seven years, *without prophet or revelation* he achieves the utmost fullness of knowledge and ineffable felicity in mystical union with his Lord. What we say is that this is a story written by a "Moslem" philosopher in the early Middle Ages in order to support the position of the rationalist philosophers that man does not stand in need of revelation in order to survive, nor indeed, in order to attain to a "mystical union with his Lord". We demonstrate why this is utter nonsense, that the atheist William Golding had it right in his *Lord of the Flies* where a group of civilized school children who are shipwrecked on an island revert back to a state of barbarism because the wick of the lantern of revelation gradually dimmed and went out for them. We argue that without the light of revelation, the eye of reason is snow blind, calling as witness the case of children who have been deprived of revelation (aka "feral" children) to prove our case, and bid our friend Alexander Dugin to take a look at these horrifying cases (five of which we provide brief histories of in a short excursus) if he wants to see what the face of what he describes as a "pre-ontological" chaos looks like. The cases are truly heart wrenching.

Précis

The last but one section, Objective Truth and the Pluralist Aftermath of its Post-Modern Critique, is a critique of postmodernist subjectivist epistemology and cultural relativism. We start off by stating that first off, because of the occultation of the divinely-appointed unimpeachable authority *(hojjat)* and the fact that we are no longer able, in many cases, properly to distinguish between right and wrong with certainty (*yaqīn*), we do not claim that Shi'a Islam has the answers. Our Imam is occulted, and we are in no better a condition epistemologically as our friends and brothers in arms are in Russia and in the West. That having been said, we go on to say, however, that because this is the case, it does not mean that we should throw tradition out wholesale, as has been done by the holy trinity of late modernity: Nietzsche, Kierkegaard, and Heidegger. And this is because of the logical impossibility of a non-foundationalist paradigm. The "exclusivism" of the Christian logos and the "universalism" of the enlightenment and liberalism are bemoaned by post-moderns. But they have yet to solve the logical contradiction that by excluding an exclusivist position, one is necessarily being exclusivist oneself. We also devote a sub-chapter against the false appeal of the Perennialists, because they, like everyone else, have not been able to see beyond the relativism of the Holy Trinity. The Eurasianists and the Grecists bemoan modernity's onslaught on tradition, but in doing so they hold fast to the most prominent hallmarks of modernity, namely, subjectivism and pluralism, which inevitably lead to secularism. We, on the other hand, arrive at the important insight that the critique of liberalism should not and cannot be directed at its foundationalism, nor even at its universalist claims (as these are epistemologically inescapable); rather, the critique should be directed at the West's desire to impose its values on others *by coercion and force*. This discussion is perhaps the heart of the essay and is not to be missed. It meets its apogee in chapter 4 on the section on Objective Truth: *Extra Ecclesiam nulla Salus* and its Alternative: the Zombification of the Soul.

And finally, we conclude the essay with an explication of the concept of *welāyat* and the principal of *tavallī* and *tabarrī* (Spiritual Affinity and the Principle of Avowal and Disavowal). What we say in this closing chapter is that those who have the ontic capacity (*qābelīa'*) of seeing that there is such a thing as right and wrong (and that it is *not* all relative), and have the capacity of being conscious of God and of accepting the message of His Apostle, and who self-surrender their will to that of God's by entering into Islam, form a community which is intent on living in accordance with God's will. This unity of purpose engenders a *spiritual affinity* between the members of the community in the sense that *they are proximate to each other in the order of creation and proximate to the Imams and to the Prophet, and therefore, by extension, to God Himself* (relative to the rest of humanity and to the other orders of being within creation). This spiritual proximity and affinity is referred to in the Shi'a literature as *welāyaʿ*.

This bond is formed and sustained on the basis of attaining to faith in the essential and fundamental religious tenet of fidelity (*towhīd*) and infidelity (*sherk*) to the covenantal commitment to the Exclusivity of God's Providential Lordship over the Social Order of His Creation, to the *lex aeterna* that is present in God, and which He communicates to His creatures through His prophets through the ages, the last of whom was Mohammad (unto whom be God's peace). Its concomitant tenet is the all-important and logically necessary principle of *tawallī* and *tabarrī*: *tawallī* (affinity; camaraderie; friendship; community – it is derived from the same root as *walīy* and *welāya*) toward those who have attained to faith in *towhīd* and are true to their sacred and communal covenant; and *berā'at* or *tabarrī* (disavowal; execration; anathematization) towards those who have failed to attain to faith in *towhīd* and have thus broken their covenant. We say that it is a logically necessary principle because in any system that is purposive, there is movement; and that movement is directed *toward* a goal and *away from* its opposite; towards *logos* and away from *anti-logos*.

Affirming a reality that we all share as members of a community who have attained to faith in a given creed or set of first principles which make up our collective and purposive constitutional order is not "racism" or ethno-centrism or nationalism, but religio-centrism, which requires the righteous act of moral exclusion against any and all who oppose the moral universe which we have attained to faith in and are certain of. It is the principle of *tawallī* and *tabarrī*, which is a necessary part of our creed. The difference is that unlike the barbarians who want to impose their "liberal" order on us by economic coercion (and when that fails, by military force), it is not incumbent on us to *impose* our beliefs on others, but merely to inform others in a peaceable manner through rational discourse that this other possibility exists.

Preamble

I first met Professor Alexander Dugin about four or five years ago. I had suggested to Mr. Nader Tālebzādeh, the Chairman of the New Horizon Conference, and to Mr. Rezā Montazamī, its Executive Director, that he would be an excellent candidate to be invited to one of the upcoming conferences. On the occasion of our first meeting, I accompanied Brother Alexander on a road trip to Qom and back, and so we had a good opportunity to get to know one another and a good preliminary exchange of views took place. Since then, I have seen Brother Alexander on three or four occasions, in Najaf and on the road to Karbalā, in Tehran, and just recently, on the occasion of the Sixth Annual New Horizon International Conference of Independent Thinkers & Artists which was held in the sacred city of Mashhad this year (2018). But unfortunately, Brother Alexander is in such high demand that we have not really had a chance to have some "quality time" together since our first road trip to Qom together. And because I had some thoughts that I considered were important for him to hear concerning his worldview and positions, I decided to put these thoughts in writing so that he could read them at his leisure if he so chooses.

It is difficult to know where to begin. From the perspective of a Shi'a thinker, one is tempted simply to dismiss Brother Alexander as just another European thinker whose mind is so confused and chock full of so many contradictions that there is no hope of success in any attempt to disentangle all of the knots within that web of confusion. After all, he claims to be a Christian, yet we see here[1] that he is a Kantian, which is another thing altogether. He is also a devotee of Martin Heidegger, and again, one cannot be a devotee of Heidegger and be devoted to Christ at one and the same time, as Heidegger wants to uproot *logos*, which is at the very heart of Christianity, and this is a project which

---

1   "A purely logical, rational model, as shown by Kant, is not capable of "grasping" an object in itself, gist of reality, which always remains inaccessible and noumenal. The "noumenon" itself keeps complete silence. Only in chaotic worlds, during "Lyapunov time," occurs the secret transition from silence to speech, from existence to nonexistence, from rational to irrational, and in reverse." Alexander Dugin, *The Fourth Political Theory*, Arktos Media, 2009.

Alexander Dugin expresses ardent support for.[2] Or his Christianity can be contrasted against his Russian nationalism and Eurasiansim; another basic incompatibility. Or again, he is a staunch anti-modernist, yet he speaks highly of the "Traditionalist" school (which is not at all traditional and is better described as the Perennialist school or movement), whereas this movement is ontologically pluralist and epistemologically subjectivist – two basic traits of modernity – while claiming, this notwithstanding, to be anti-modern. It is good to join the struggle against the onslaught of modernity on traditional values, but first, let us get the basics right. And so, like I said, it is tempting to be dismissive; but I have too much affection for Alexander, who I know to be a person of great personal integrity with a pious soul and heart, and I have too much respect for his vast intellectual capacities. And so, the criticisms which I present, while they are radical and in our view deeply undermine the foundations of his intellectual edifice, are offered in the spirit of friendship and as constructive criticism to the leader of a movement which we consider to be highly valuable, and to be foremost in our alliance against the hegemonic forces of evil which pervade the whole world around us today.

As my friend Alexander Dugin has correctly pointed out in his book *The Fourth Political Theory*, Communism and Fascism and National Socialism have been defeated by Liberalism. We agree with Professor Dugin that Liberalism is ideologically bankrupt, based on its actions, which form the reality of what Liberalism actually is in practice, and which reality in turn undermines the theory with which it is at radical variance. We also believe that it is ideologically bankrupt, being a profane and imperfect substitute for the world order which God intends for us. What we are referring to is not just the foreign policy of the Liberal Order which is allied with the Wahhabist heretics who have a stranglehold on Arabia and allied with the Zionist entity, whose crimes in the open-air prison of the Gaza Strip have been made to pale in comparison with the criminal actions of the Wahhabeasts and their Atlanticist enablers in the Yemen; but also to the economic realities in the "First" World (First on the road to Hell), where the people "democratically" choose to be exploited by less than 1% of the population, which continues to own and control the vast majority of the resources in these countries, and where their systematic financial

---

2 Towards the end of his *Fourth Political Theory*.

Preamble

malfeasance in Wall Street and the City of London has brought all of the European countries who are part of the NATO alliance to the brink of bankruptcy and kept them there, waiting for the Big Bubble to burst into flames and consume that civilization like the Ouroboros serpent eating its own tail.

And we agree with this apt summary by the erudite scholar Michael O'Meara that "the liberal today loudly proclaims the "rights of man," but has not a word for the rights of communities, the rights of peoples, the rights of nations, the rights of states, or what Catholics once referred to as "the rights of God." Of these rights, whose integrity resists unregulated markets and the atomizing forces of bourgeois individualism, the liberal accords no recognition." Indeed, *we* (in the besieged Shi'a citadel) still ardently affirm the rights of God (*haqq ol-'Āh*), and are in the same camp as Dugin, O'Meara and the European New Right (henceforth, ENR) when it comes to community rights trumping individual rights. Thus, when we offer a critique of Alexander Dugin and Alain de Benoist and the ENR, it is because we agree with their diagnosis and even with their prognosis of what will become of liberal democracy, and consider them to be allies in the struggle to defeat the evil hegemonic impetus of what is left of this dying zombie-giant.

What we disagree on is the cure to the ailment and on the way forward out of the dead-end that the Liberal Order has landed all of us in. The solution that we proffer arises from the wellspring of an integral ideological system which integrates all first principles (be they creedal, theological or philosophical) into a system of social interaction and identity which integrates political philosophy with all of the most fundamental religious and axiological tenets which are the creedal basis of Shi'a Islam. As such, our critiques of individual aspects of the big picture will necessarily take a very different and more radical approach to the issues at hand. But irrespective of these radical differences (and there is a huge chasm that separates us, as we shall see presently), we consider the work of Alexander Dugin and Alain de Benoist and the European New Right as that which is closest to our own take (in terms of the deconstruction only) and as that which has the most merit and is most worthy of intellectual engagement in the field of those thinkers who are talking and writing about the big picture. (Those Traditional Catholics such as my good friend E. Michael Jones and *Sede Vacantists* such as Bishop Richard

The European New Right - A Shia Response

Williamson also offer excellent critiques of modernity (I am thinking especially of Bishop Williamson's exposition and explication of the *Pascendi* Papal encyclical and its critique of "the Copernican Revoluiton" which Kant wrought in philosophy with his neumenon/phenomenon distinction); and the positive edifice which they offer as an alternative is much more comprehensive and much more rooted in tradition and revelation; but alas, the institution of the Catholic Church is intellectually if not spiritually bankrupt and has become yet another Zombie[3] as manifested by the wound which it self-inflicted during the proceeding of the Second Vatican Council of 1962-65 and the papal encyclical which succeeded it; and as such, it is incapable of producing anything of lasting value and, like Liberal Democracy and the Pax Americana of Bretton Woods of 1944 (and the privatization of money creation before it in Jekyll Island which Congress passed and the president signed into law in that portentous December of 1913), our concern must be to maneuver our relations with them in such a way as to bring them down in their own footprint so as to avoid the least amount of collateral damage. We might even try to prevail upon the BBC to report the scheduled demolitions a half hour before the events, like they were kind enough to do for Building 7 of the World Trade Center on 9/11/2001. Oh, yes. *That*, pilgrims, is the magnitude of the unmitigated audacity of their satanic mirth. "That's what's the deal we're dealing in", to quote the late, great, rude, crude, and socially unacceptable Frank Zappa.

We are approaching the work of Alexander Dugin and Alain de Benoist from the perspective of an entirely different civilization. As such, we must first establish certain first principles which are the basis of the worldview of this civilization in order to be able to refer our arguments and criticisms to these principles and ensure that our readers are in a position to follow what we have said and the bases and footings on which the edifice of our argument is built. And so, our negative criticism will invariably be intermingled with a positive presentation of the alternative(s) provided by the Shi'a tradition. As such, this essay will necessarily also be an explication of traditional Shi'a metaphysics, presented from a comparative and, inevitably, a somewhat proselytizing perspective.

---

3   A man without a soul; an amoral being; a man who is unable to distinguish and choose between right and wrong.

Preamble

And as a last word, we would like to add that one of the major criticisms which Professor Dugin readily admits to (but which remains a major weakness nevertheless), is the fact that his position as well as that of Alain de Benoist and that of everyone else on the European New Right lacks a *systematic* and *comprehensive* framework. You will notice this simply by contrasting their positions with the expositions which we provide of Islam's systematic, comprehensive and integral worldview, approach and solution to the greatest issues that are facing us in the world today. This is an important distinction, because we all agree that the West has failed in so far as what it has to offer is the liberal order, which is nothing but putting the ugly head of secular humanism on what was left of the rationalist/ universalist body after the Reformation and the Enlightenment and the Age of Reason had their way with it. Ok; the West has failed. But it is not enough to say that the West has failed and then not be able to provide a better solution.

The reason the Islamic Revolution succeeded where the Egyptian one failed is because the clerisy were able to inform the vision of the masses of *an alternative*, and it was only after Imam Khomeini was confident that the consciousness of this alternative had reached the level of critical mass (and that consequently, for example, the army would quickly join the protesters and would not shoot at them), that he determined that the country was ripe for an insurrection. The Occupy Wall Street movement was on to something important, but when all they could do is shout "We are the 99%" when in fact they were less than 1% of the population who were even *aware* that they were being taken to the cleaners by Uncle $cam, then it was obvious to me that they had no chance of success whatsoever.

It is equally obvious to me that none of the good people involved in the struggle against the hegemonic forces of the New World Order have any chance whatsoever of attaining to a critical mass consciousness on a reform or revolutionary program on which they have a consensus of opinion or near-consensus. And this is because the only force that can even rise up to defeat this evil force will be sent by Providence. I am sorry, but you are not the 99%; you are the 1%. This is what we believe, and as you read through the pages of this essay, you should bear in mind that it is an alternative thesis that we are proposing, and you should judge it as such in terms of its ability better to predict future outcomes, as well as its potential for bringing about real change. And perhaps you will not have any choice, because with the Empire of Chaos bombing the MENA back to the stone age and Europe receiving all the Islamicate-trash economic migrants and not being able to do anything about it because your governments have been taken over by the ZOG hegemon, then it would seem that Shi'a Islam would be the only remaining way to civilize them. (Needless to say, we are against Moslems emigrating to non-Moslem lands for economic or any other purposes.)

1. *Ex Oriente Lux*

The Islamic Revolution of 1979 as the Antithesis of the Collapse of the West's *Grand Récit*

But before proceeding to that explication, let us first say that Alexander Dugin is mistaken in stating that there were only three political theories in the 20th century (and that what he proposes, therefore, is the fourth). As the *Soixont-Huitards* were doing their thing in Paris, and as the esteemed Alain de Benoist founded the European 'New Right' movement in France with the establishment of GRECE (Research and Study Group for European Civilization) in 1968, Imām Khomeinī (at the time, he was known as Grand Ayatollah Khomeinī) was teaching his theory of *velāyat-e faqīh* or the guardianship-type governance of the Shi'a doctors of sacred jurisprudence cum theologians cum theosophers while in exile in the seminary at Najaf. The notes of these lectures which were delivered in 1968 and 1969 were redacted by his students and presented to Imām Khomeinī for his review. The reviewed and amended version of these redacted notes were eventually published a year later in early 1970. Less than a decade later, the world was changed by the Islamic Revolution of 1978-79. I say the world, because not only did the Islamic Revolution of Iran change the Islamic world, and Iran, which has always been its intellectual if not spiritual capital; but it changed the whole world. It woke the world up from its secular humanist daydream. Indeed, it was Imam Khomeinī's movement which woke the West up from the secular human belief that man is free to do as he pleases.

أَيَحْسَبُ الْإِنسَانُ أَن يُتْرَكَ سُدًى

[75:36] [What?!] Does man, then, think that he is to be left to himself to go about at will?

Brother Alexander and the ENR have (mostly) arrived at the right conclusions in terms of their deconstruction of the liberal order, but from the wrong path. And that is why their theories and movement will not be able to withstand the test of time. And even your prescriptions are generally correct. You have finally arrived at the position that what should be done is to adopt the left's position on labor and environmental laws and on social justice, and the right's position on traditional values, the importance of family, religion and hierarchy, and the rights of God and of the community being given priority over the rights of the individual, who, after all is said and done, can only grow out of the seedbed of community. In other words, you have arrived at a position that Shi'a Islam (and decidedly not Sunni Islam) has held consistently for fourteen centuries. So far, so good. But because your whole approach is philosophical and not religious, and even if it were religious, it would still be encumbered by the problems of Christianity – because of this, your methodological error, which has led to errors in your ideological positions, your theory has failed to take into account this most basic fact of the seismic event that 1979 was, even though Shi'a Islam's positions on social justice and traditional values is exactly and not approximately what your position is, and has anticipated it by nothing less than fourteen centuries.

Michael O'Meara claims that the only historical cases conforming to the New Right's imperial idea have been those of Rome, Byzantium, the Hohenstaufens, and the Hapsburgs, and that in these "traditionalist empires", cultural, linguistic, national, and social boundaries did not coincide (as in a nation) nor were they subordinate to a single model of life (as the *pax americana* dictates), but that, rather, their unity "rested on an affiliation to a common ideal, upon whose basis their differences were integrated". We cannot comment on the extent to which this is the case, but can state that while the immediate ambit and reach of the Islamic Revolution is limited to the borders of Iran which acts as the Shi'a citadel, its spiritual sovereignty and authority are based on the principle of *ordo ducit ad Deum* (an order leading to God), and thus shine bright outside of its Westphalian borders for those whose eyes are open and can see *ex oriente lux* (the light from the East). As such, its sovereignty and authority are universal, eternal, sacred, and salvific.

It was in this same watershed year of the Revolution of 1979 (The year 1400 of the Islamic lunar calendar) that Lyotard's *La Condition Postmoderne* appeared; and as the roots of the Islamic Revolution took hold and the first adumbrations of the Islamic Republic began to crystalize in the East, the postmodern critique of modernity and of the whole Western project began to take hold in a parallel and seemingly unrelated procedure in the West. Jean-François Lyotard,

1. Ex Oriente Lux

the first and perhaps most influential philosopher to interpret the post-modern condition, describes it in terms of the collapse of the *grand récit*, or of the Great Narrative coursing through the discourse of modernity. It is the thesis of this writer that the Revolution of 1979, flawed as it inevitably is, is the only possible antithesis to the West's "metanarrative collapse" – Nietzsche's Will to Power, Heidegger's uprooting of *logos* in favor of *chaos*, Kierkegaard's rejection of institutionalized religion in favor of a radical individualism based on an irrational Leap of Faith, nor yet Brother Dugin's Fourth Political Theory – none of these are able to withstand what William Connolly has called reason's "perpetual process of self-critique" absent the only true and valid revelation that is the Final Testament of the Quran, which superseded the New Testament fifteen lunar centuries ago.

Brother Alexander correctly states that postmodernity cannot be transcended "without appeal to something that has been [in existence] prior to the reason of its decay." He goes on to say that "we should resort to philosophies other than Western", and that "If we seek well, we can find the real forms of such intellectual traditions in archaic societies, as well as in Eastern theology." In an editorial footnote added by the excellent editors at Arktos Media to Alexander Dugin's *Fourth Political Theory*, we learn that in his book *The End of Our Time* (1924), Nikolai Berdyaev (1874-1948), the influential Russian millenarian mystic and political philosopher, prophesied the imminent end of liberalism and humanism, and the return of what he termed a New Middle Ages, which would include a return to civilizations based upon religion and mysticism. Well – surprise! – the Islamic Revolution of Iran of 1978-79 is nothing less than the fulfillment of this visionary prophecy.

To be sure, when we say that the crystallization of the values and ideals of the Islamic Revolution under the constitutional law of the Islamic Republic are taking place "in a parallel and seemingly unrelated procedure" to the collapse of the Grand Narrative in the West, we do not mean to imply that therefore, the Islamic Republic has stumbled upon the solution to all of the problems of the East and of the West and of humanity at large. By no means. First and foremost because the good people who are holding the reins of power in the Islamic Republic – who are surrounded by a tidal wave of apple polishers and hypocrites (who are worse than unbelievers) and idiots – must first clean out their own barn of such pigs before they can start to set an example for the rest of the world, starting with the Department of Justice, whose corruption is at the root of the intractability of many of the problems that we face. I'm sorry, but it is what it is; but at least it is better than the situation in some of the countries in the West where I have heard that one can actually *marry* such pigs in brothels who enjoy the sanction of their legislative plenums (and I am not talking about pigs in a metaphorical sense here, but ones with all that good back-bacon)! But the more important reason is that even if we here in the besieged Shi'a citadel were able to get our act together and were to act as real exemplary models for the rest of the world, the situation would still not be tenable, just as it is untenable in the West. And this, as I told Alexander in the conference in Mashhad, is because mankind's rebellion against God's order obtained in the world of those who attained to faith in Islam, just as it obtained in Christendom (the main reason being their failure to heed the words of warning of the Final Prophet, may God's peace be with him and with the purified and immaculate members of his House); so that subsequently, eleven of the twelve Imams who were sent as divine guides to humanity after the passing of the Prophet as a grace and as a mercy from God, were martyred by agents of the Omayyad and Abbasid tyrants. And eventually the situation got so bad that the twelfth and final Divine Guide was taken up by God and is being kept in a state of physical occultation, so that our condition is beyond repair absent the advent of that Divine Guide and absent the Second Coming of the Christ Jesus, son of Mary (unto all of whom be God's peace). All we can do is to work to the best of our ability in the seemingly Sisyphusian task of attempting to establish God's will on Earth as it is in Heaven in the absence of the Imam al-Mahdī (the Guided One) and in the absence of the Christ Jesus, all the while being conscious of the impossibility of our task. The *consciousness* of this impossibility will prevent us from falling into the error and heresy of Pelagianism and what Eric Voeglin famously characterized as "the imminantization of the Eschaton"; imminantizing the advent of the Savior by the works of man (like the political Judaism of the Zionists) instead of waiting with active patience (*entezār*) for Providence's will to be accomplished in the fullness of God's own good time. But the *function* of this impossibility – the impossibility of having different poles live as different "humanities" in peace with each other – an impossibility which will become more and more obviated as we spiral down ever steeper into the vortex at the end of history (or into the

1. Ex Oriente Lux

"momentous historical turn", to use Ayatollah Khāmeneī's famous phrase) – the function of this impossibility is to awaken humanity from its absurd, self-assured and arrogant humanism, and to engender in mankind that original spiritual sense of dependence on a Higher Power, and subsequent need for Guidance from Above. To awaken, in other words, the original religious consciousness and impetus in mankind, and to humble his arrogance, so that he can better conform himself to reality, so that he can find salvation through God and the message that He has sent through His Apostles. The impossibility, in other words, acts as yet another Portal of Grace.[1] But from our point of view, the difference between the impossibility of *this* self-critical Shi'a position and its active awaiting (*entezār*), and the impossibility of our Western brothers who are sitting on the fence or still going around in circles, is that the former posture is salvific and will have eternal rewards in the hereafter whereas the latter's is as spiritually sterile as the zombies and spiritual chimaeras who gaily parade themselves in New Orleans on Mardi Gras every year, or in the Castro District in San Francisco or in the various capitals of the modern Sodoms and Gomorrahs of the West on Gay Pride Day.

---

[1] For a fuller discussion of this topic, see chapter 11. (From Multipolarity back to Unipolarity).

2. The Metaphysics of Chaos

At the beginning of the essay entitled *The Metaphysics of Chaos* Alexander Dugin defines *logos* as "the logical order of being" and, following Heidegger, states that "modern European philosophy began with the concept of *logos*" and that "All the potentialities and the principles laid in this logocentric way of thinking have by now been thoroughly explored, exposed and abandoned by philosophers" so that "this concept became fully exhausted". Alexander Dugin then goes on to say that "chaos is something opposite to logos, its absolute alternative", and that this concept has been neglected throughout the history of Western philosophy in favor of the discredited logos.

A little later, we learn that the European philosophy which was "based on the logocentric principle ... of exclusion ... [which] corresponds strictly to the masculine attitude and reflects a patriarchal, authoritative, vertical, and hierarchical order of being and knowledge... has come to an end", and that we must therefore "consider another road for thought, [that is] not in the logocentric, phallocentric, hierarchical and exclusivist way." In other words, "the most important and brilliant European philosophers (such as Friedrich Nietzsche and Martin Heidegger) began to suspect that logos was fast approaching its end... [and that] we are living in the time of the end of logocentric philosophy, and approaching... something else."

So far, we are in basic agreement with Brothers Nietzsche, Heidegger, and Dugin. We do not necessarily agree with their definitional framework or with their specific characterizations of the issue, but that is not important at this juncture. We agree with their diagnosis, as well as with their prescription, or more precisely, their proscription, which is to jettison the entirety of the Western philosophical tradition overboard. But the *reason* why we agree with the proscription differs from our fellow pilgrims. They reason that the Greeks reasoned incorrectly (and therefore, all those who followed them, especially Plato and Aristotle, and Augustine and Aquinas, *also* reasoned incorrectly). Let us not get into the broad classifications of the supposed errors, such as referentialism and nominalism at this juncture; suffice it to say that we agree that the entire Western philosophical tradition got off on the wrong track. And we would add that the entire *Islamic* philosophico-mystical tradition, from Eben Sīnā (Avicenna) to Fārābī to Eben 'Arabi to Sohrevardī to Mollā Sadrā and Allāme Mohammad Hosayn Tabātabāī – all of these got it wrong too. So they reason that all these people reasoned incorrectly, and that they should *reason* in a different way, namely, correctly! Where we differ concerning the prescription is that we are with the logical positivists with respect to the efficacy of reason, or more accurately, the absence of any efficacy for reason, when it comes to the metaphysical or trans-physical realm; the realm which the Quran refers to as *al-ghayb* which is commonly translated as "[the world or domain of] the unseen" but which Mohammad Asad, may God rest his blessed soul, masterfully translated as "the domain which is beyond the ken of ordinary understanding". In other words, we are with A.J. Ayer, W. Quine, and especially Ludwig Wittgenstein when he said, "Whereof one cannot speak, thereof one must be silent."

Strange bedfellows, I hear you say; and I would agree. But we only agree with them with respect to their implacable insight that where reason's calipers do not have any purchase, then one should put reason aside and see what other instruments or faculties are available (if any). They could not find any other instruments or faculty, and so they reasonably limited their search to where the spotlight of reason shines, which is downward onto the material plane and no higher. Where they were mistaken is to then claim that reason's spotlight is the only place where a light shines, and so proceeded to make fools of themselves. To put it slightly less delicately but more to the point, reason *reasons* that the trans-physical realm or the realm of *al-ghayb* is a realm where the angel of reason fears to tread; and thus reason bows to true revelation when it encounters it, knowing that it speaks of a realm concerning which it has no jurisdiction. Reason *reasons* that the trans-physical realm is dark to it as a faculty of intellection and understanding, and that a failure to bow to revelation with respect to basic questions concerning being and its nature will result in just more verbal, that is to say, philosophical diarrhea. And so, where we differ with our fellow travelers Brothers Nietzsche, Heidegger, and Dugin is that when reason has taken us to the edge of the Abyss (to use Nietzsche's word), *we* see the limitations of the faculty of intellection which can only think in terms of *discrete concepts* and *finite entities*, and follow reason's bidding to open the door of that *other* special faculty of intellection known as revelation, and enter through that

2. The Metaphysics of Chaos

door in order to be able to see beyond the veil of reason; whereas our fellow travelers are still standing at the edge of the abyss arguing about what to do and where to go, and doing so with that same faculty which *itself* has told them that "this *logocentric* way of thinking has by now been thoroughly explored, exposed and abandoned." Yet they refuse to abandon it, and go on and on about a pre-ontological chaos, a will to power, and an irrational leap of faith of the supra-individuated individual, in the case of Brother Kierkegaard.

If they did abandon it as their reason bids them so to do, and if they followed us through that door of revelation which is not the Old Testament or the New Testament, which have been superseded, but the Final Testament which is the Quran; then this is what they would find. In other words, what we say to the anti-modernists is that it is all well and good to inveigh against modernity and maintain some nebulous connection with the Christian tradition, but let us not forget that ultimately, the Enlightenment thinkers were *right* to insist that revelation be subject to the rigorous examination of reason; where they erred was in the overplus of the scope which they afforded reason, holding it in an irrationally high level of esteem in terms of its efficacy and competence, which is why they rightly rejected Greco-Pauline Christianity as irrational (as we shall prove presently), but continued their hyper-rational sweep to include *all* religions, thereby not affording the Islamic revelation the scrutiny that it richly deserves.

3. Finitude and the Tripartite Proof[1]

The full name for this chapter is Finitude and the Tripartite Proof for the Existence of God, for His Utterly Transcendent Nature, and His Unicity. What will follow in this chapter is a simple rational proof which not only proves the existence of God as the Creator of the world, but proves that his nature is utterly transcendent and that He is infinite and eternal, and as such, must necessarily be unitary and unique. It is a very simple proof and, in keeping with the Quranic methodology, relies on common sense or that which is or should be obvious to all. But because certain types of people have a penchant for complicating things out of all due proportion and for unnecessary "sophistication" (and because of the baggage of the Greek philosophical tradition which was imported by the Abbāsids into the Islamic world in order to combat the righteous teachings of Islam as taught by the Purified and Immaculate members of the Household of the Prophet (the *ahl al-bayt*), who did not recognize the legitimacy of the Abbāsids to rule over the community of Moslems), a whole "Islamic" philosophical tradition developed in parallel with the teachings of the *ahl al-bayt*, and this tradition which goes back to Eben Sīnā (Avicenna) and Fārābī and can be traced through Eben 'Arabī and Sohrevardī to Mollā Sadrā and Mīr Dāmād and the School of Isfahān, is just as confused and at variance with reality as is its Christian counterpart (as we will attempt to demonstrate in the sections which follow).

The earlier and original tradition was dominant in the early centuries of Islam and was present strongly in the thought and outlook of Ayatollah Borujerdī, who was the greatest Source of Religio-Legal Emulation (*marja'-e taqlīd*) prior to the Imam Khomeinī era. This truly Islamic and anti-philosophical tradition includes all of the early luminaries of Shi'a Islam, from Shaykh Mofīd and his two students, Shaykh ot-Tā'efa Nasīr od-Dīn Tūsī and Seyyed Mortadā, to Allāme Hellī and Allāme Mohammad Bāqer Majlesī, all the way up to Ayatollah Borujerdī. It predominated Shi'a theological thought from

---

1 Credit for the collation and summarization of this tripartite proof, which is gleaned from the rational proofs and arguments to be found in the hadīth corpus of the Immaculate Imams, unto all of whom be God's peace and blessings, goes to Master Mahdī Nasīrī, Magister Extraordinaire.

its inception, based on the teachings of the Prophet and the Imams, and was dominant throughout all of the early and middle centuries of Islam. But gradually, philosophical accretions and syncretisms seeped in, so that in the last Islamic century, the philosophical and mystical tradition represented by Mollā Sadrā and Allāme Tabātabāī, who was its latest representative, came to dominate the seminaries.

Thus, the difference between what is known as *kalām* or Islamic theology (in its broadest sense) and philosophy used to be that *kalām* referred to the science of dogmatics and apologetic theology, whereas *falsafa* or Islamic philosophy was a science that was based on the dictates of reason and logic and did not partake of the revealed sources of knowledge, i.e. the Quran and the *hadīth* report corpus. But as time progressed, this distinction became less and less pronounced in favor of the methodological approach of the latter – a bias which sharpened in the Post-Classical era of Islamic philosophy and the so-called Iranian cultural renaissance of the 17th century led by Mollā Sadrā (d. 1640) and his theosophical synthesis.

In any event, the simple rational proof that follows is all that one needs to know about God's essence or nature, and is in fact all that *can* be known about this. From the perspective of the original Islamic and anti-philosophical teachings, this position is not, therefore, "irrational" as some have falsely accused it of being. Rather, it is a much *more* rational position as it uses reason to the extent of its capacity, and leaves out all of the philosophical speculation, which can never amount to anything more than just that: speculation. Whereas we do not have to live in a state of speculative uncertainty, as the Quran was revealed to us by God precisely in order to bring us out of this state of confusion concerning the metaphysical world or the world which the Quran refers to as the *ālam al-ghayb* or as the domain that is beyond the ken of ordinary human perception. In this important sense, then, Islamic monotheism also means unity and integrality of thought and worldview, and the philosophical tradition is anything but that (almost by definition).

* * *

3. Finitude and the Tripartite Proof

Earlier we posited that an important limitation of the faculty of *rational* intellection was that it can only think in terms of *discrete concepts* and *finite entities*. Let us now apply this insight to a proof for the existence of God, which at one and the same time also provides for a proof of God's absolute[2] transcendence, as well as of His singularity or unicity.

This same characteristic of finitude which is the stock in trade of reason, as we just discussed above, means that the phenomena of this world are discrete, bounded entities, which are therefore *quantifiable* and locatable in space and in time. And contrary to Parmenides who believed that the world was eternal, the quantifiability of the phenomena of the world and of the world itself means that such phenomena and the world cannot be eternal. Let us see why this is the case.

Let us assume for the sake of the argument that the world is infinite and is *not* bounded (as Parmenides, Eben 'Arabī and Molla Sadrā, among others, would have it). Now let us take away a part of it; say, the solar system. By so doing, would we or would we not have reduced the universe by that amount? The answer is obvious: we would have, for otherwise, we would not have taken anything away. (To say that the universe has *not* been diminished is tantamount to saying that the solar system had not been taken away, whereas we stated that for the purpose of this exercise, it had.[3]) On the other hand, if we grant that it *has* been diminished – and we must grant this – then what this means is that the universe has the capacity of being diminished or is diminishable. This capacity in any given subject means that it is finite and not infinite, as something that is infinite cannot be diminished, and anything that can be added to or subtracted from is finite and quantifiable, i.e. it is not beyond quantifiability.

---

2   The Shi'a position is that His transcendence is absolute with the exception that we can know that He exists and know that we cannot know any more about His essence. Our knowledge concerning His essence, in other words, stops just short of agnosticism. But there are many things that we can and do know about His attributes due to his Quranic self-disclosure.

3   In other words, if someone made the objection that the universe was not thereby diminished, we would respond that such a person has not understood the meaning of diminishment, as he is equating that which has been diminished with that which has not, and saying that the two are the same.

(And it follows that any being or entity that is quantifiable and has number will continue to be quantifiable and be subject to enumeration irrespective of the magnitude of its quantity, so that it is impossible for such a finite, quantifiable being to issue an *infinite* being, no matter how great the latter's magnitude.)

So now that it has been established that the world and everything within it are finite, discrete, quantifiable entities, it also follows by definition that such entities had and have a beginning in time, because they are not infinite or unbounded by time. In other words, there is a point in time for all finite entities whereat they came into being, before which point they did not exist. (This is the very definition of having a beginning in time.)

The next question is: Does something that does not exist and then comes into existence do so on its own? The answer to this question must be negative, because nothing happens without a cause. There is not a single thing in this world that happens without a cause. This is a matter of simple observation and a matter of the very definition of cause and effect: there can be no effect without a cause. And likewise, every created being has a creator; there can be no created entity without there being a creator to create it. Therefore, if the world and everything within it are not timeless but are created, then there must necessarily be a Creator who created them. (To our mind, and to the mind of the ancient philosophers of Greece, and to the minds of the schoolmen in the high middle ages and before, these matters, of any effects necessarily having a cause, and of any being which is a created being having a creator, are both statements which are obvious to a rational being and do not stand in need of any further explanation or rational demonstration and support. It is only the minds which have been infected with the pathogenic humanist bacillus of modern skepsis which demure from acquiescing to these obvious logical facts. We will talk about this mental paralysis a little further down in this same section.)

Now if the Being Who created this world is of the same kind as the world itself, it too would be finite and bounded, which would mean that it too was created; which in turn would mean that it was created and therefore not the Creator, (and would thus also stand in need of a Creator); and this logical progression would proceed in this manner

3. Finitude and the Tripartite Proof

ad infinitum into what is called an infinite regress. And as such an infinite regress is not capable of producing a Creator that is of the same kind as the created entity or entities, it therefore follows that the Creator must necessarily be different in kind. And that the kind of entity which the Creator is, must, by the rule of exclusion, be an unbounded, infinite and unquantifiable Being (because if this Being is not finite, it must necessarily be infinite).

So we have by now established that there must be a Creator, and that He must be infinite. And when we realize that the Creator must necessarily be infinite, we also realize that this means that there can only be a single entity of this kind or species, because if there were more than one, then that entity would not be unbounded and would be finite and quantifiable, which would mean that it was created, and so on. (It is not possible to conceive of two infinite entities side by side or one alongside the other; it is a logical impossibility.)

The Quran refers to this singular and unique quality of God's as *ahad* and *samad*:

قُلْ هُوَ اللَّهُ أَحَدٌ

اللَّهُ الصَّمَدُ

[112:1] Say: "He is the One (*ahad*) God (one in the sense of being a singularity, un-numbered, and utterly unique)":

[112:2] "God the Eternally Self-Sufficient and Absolute (the All-Embracing Uncaused Cause of All Being Who stands in need of none and of Whom all are in need) (*as-Samad*).

Elsewhere, Allāh provides the following corrective to those who mistakenly believe that He can be described in terms of concepts and categories:

سُبْحَانَهُ وَتَعَالَىٰ عَمَّا يَقُولُونَ عُلُوًّا كَبِيرًا

[17:43] Limitless is He in His glory, and sublimely, immeasurably exalted above anything that men may ascribe [to Him by way of definition].

(The exception, of course, are those concepts and categories, and those attributes which He provides concerning Himself in his Quranic self-disclosure, as stated earlier; the utter transcendence refers to His essence.)

Thus, it is this Being who is utterly different Who is "the Creator", and the entirety of the order of Creation and all of the beings within it are "the created".

* * *

Here ends the one and only proof for the existence of God the Creator. This proof is derived from *hadīth* reports within the Shi'a *hadīth* corpus and is at one and the same time a proof for His nature as being utterly different to that of the nature of finite or created beings, as well as being a proof of His unicity or singularity. To put it slightly differently, what this proof establishes is that logic dictates that there must necessarily be a Creator (no "leap of faith is required"); that the Creator is not of the same kind or nature as His created beings (no anthropomorphism); and that there can only be one creator (no polytheism or Chalcedonian mystagogery).

Let us say two words concerning this proof before we move on from the theoretical realm and apply its significance to the world in which we live and to our cosmology and anthropology.

The first point is addressed to those who are in the habit of philosophizing everything to death; to the sophists and skeptics among us who cannot see a simple, rational and logical proof when it is staring them in the face. God is well aware of these types, and mocks them, saying,

كَلَّا إِنَّا خَلَقْنَاهُم مِّمَّا يَعْلَمُونَ

[70:39] By no means! For, behold, We have created them out of that which they know [only too well]!

And then

وَإِن يَرَوْا كِسْفًا مِّنَ السَّمَاءِ سَاقِطًا يَقُولُوا سَحَابٌ مَّرْكُومٌ

3. Finitude and the Tripartite Proof

[52:44] And yet, if they [who refuse to see the truth] were to see part of the sky falling down, they would [only] say, "[It is nothing but] a heap of clouds, piled up!"

And so, one must be very cautious concerning the overplus of sophistication and casuistry that the ever more sophisticated philosophy of modern times has become, as it is a veritable quagmire of quicksand.

The second point has to do with what this proof demonstrates that God is *not*. As He is infinite and thus utterly different and "Sublimely and immeasurably exalted above anything that men may ascribe [to Him by way of definition]", then it is obvious that saying that a man is also God is a logical absurdity. And religion is that which we are "bound to" as our way of life, and I am sorry, but not a single iota of my religion and way of life is absurd, let alone that which resides at its very core. And no, no matter how many times one says that the incarnation and the trinity is a "mystery" and a "paradox", these will not take away from the fact that a mystery is one thing, and a contradiction and logical absurdity is something very different. A paradox is something that evades rational understanding, whereas a logical absurdity is patently obvious on its surface. One can continue to say one is *actually* three, and that three is *actually* one until one is blue in the face, but we say that one is one and three is three, and never the twain shall meet! (Imam Rezā states in *at-Towhīd* that there are only [two types of being:] God and His creation; and that there is no third [type of being such as a created being or man who is also, somehow, God] between them; and that there is nothing other than these two [ontological forms]. Imam Ja'far as-Sādeq also states that "there is no third [species of being or ontological form] other than that of God and His creation."[4]

And the pantheists and those who subscribe to the Spinozan view of the world or to Eben 'Arabī's pantheistic *wahdat al-wujūd* (or Unicity of Being) thesis or to Mollā Sadrā's "transcendental wisdom" (*hekmat-e mote'ālīe*) should note that this proof does away with that monist error as well, as the proof clearly demonstrates that there are two categories of being and not one: the first which is comprised

---

4   *Behār* 4:161

solely of God, who is uncreated, and unitary – the singularity; the One (*al-Ahad*), and the Eternally Self-Sufficient and Absolute (*as-Samad*); and then there is everything that is other than God, i.e. everything in the world of creation, including the angles and the jinn and mankind, all of which are created, and who owe their reality to the Creator, and whose reality, therefore, is neither self-sufficient, nor sustainable without God's will; and is thus a second tier order of reality.

4. Elaborations on the Proof of Finitude[1]

Let us now take a closer look at some of the implications of the Proof of Finitude and elaborate on its tenets and implications by way of *hadīth* reports and commentaries on these reports.

Apophatic Theology

Imam Ali provides the following hermeneutical exegesis (*ta'wīl*) of the word *as-Samad* (which is recorded in the *Jāme' ol-Akhbār*):

> The *ta'wīl* of *as-Samad* is [that God is] neither a noun or a body; there is nothing that is a likeness of Him, nor does he have a face or visage; there is nothing that can be said to be a similitude of Him, nor is He limited by any bound; He does not have position or location, nor does He have any quality; He cannot be said to be here or there, nor can He be described as being full or empty. He is not in motion, neither is He still; He is neither light, nor darkness; He is neither material nor spiritual. No place can be said to be empty of Him, nor can it be said that he is encompassed by a given place or situation. He has no colority, no odor, nor can He be encompassed by [the faculty of] the heart – none of these [attributes] pertain to Him.[2]

And in the *Nahj ol-Balāgha*, the Imam adds concerning the word *as-Samad* that neither is God within any object, nor is He outside any.[3] Elsewhere, he states that "anything that can be conceptualized [concerning God or ascribed to him intellectually], God is contrary

---

1   All of the hadīth entries quoted in these subsections are taken from Sheykh Hasan Mīlānī's indispensable *Farātar az Erfān*. Much of my commentaries on the hadīth reports in these sections are similarly indebted to him.

2   *Behār* 3:230, taken from the Jāme' ol-Akhbār.

3   Some Sunni commentators have said that *as-Samad* means that God is something that is not empty but full. This is an error that Imam Ali corrects in the above commentary, where God's attribute of *as-Samad* is explained to mean that He neither has an inside nor an outside (and can therefore neither be full or empty). The Sunni interpretation implies that God is like an object that can be full or empty, which means that He can be located in space, which means that he is finite. Of course, the Hanbalis and Zāheris and and Ash'aris even interpret verses where the Quran talks about God's "hand" literally, not realizing that this is a patent error.

to it.[4] In a clear explication of the fact that the essence of God can be understood only in apophatic terms, Imam as-Sādeq says that "*Towhīd* (the primary creedal tenet of Islam; the belief in the unicity of God) means that anything [= any attribute] which you might conceivably attribute to yourself, you [should] deny [its applicability] to your Lord and Sustainer (*rabb*)."[5] He continues his apophatic explication by stating that "Anything which is present in creation cannot be found in its Creator; and anything that is possible within and concerning creation is not possible concerning its Creator."[6] He then asks, "How is it possible to apply to Him that which He has originated and created?"[7]

The sacred essence of God can never be comprehended by human intelligence, which does not have the intellectual let alone ontic capacity to "take in" God's essence. For one thing, human comprehension is an intellectual process which involves "taking in" or "wrapping" one's mind "around" a given subject, by which expressions are meant encompassing all sides of the issue, so as to be able to situate it in its proper spacial, temporal, and intellectual context; whereas God, being infinite and eternal, cannot be contained by such processes. Thus, the proper understanding of the sacred essence of God is one which ultimately cannot be attained, and is one which must be thought of apophatically, i.e. in terms of what it isn't.

Imam Sajjād, the Fourth Imam of the Shi'a, has stated that "God has not allowed a single human being to have any more knowledge concerning His essence other than that this essence is unknowable. He considers those who think of their knowledge of Him as incomplete to be praiseworthy and considers this [epistemological posture concerning] knowledge of Him to be [a form of] gratitude."[8]

Imam Ali has stated: "Praise be unto God Who has created deliberation and contemplation [concerning God and His nature or essence in such a way as] to be incapable of understanding naught but His existence."[9]

---

4   *Behār* 4:253; and *Ehtejāj* 1:201.
5   *Behār*, 4:264.
6   *At-Towhīd*, p. 40; *Behār* 4:230.
7   *At-Towhīd*, p. 40; *Behār* 4:230.
8   *Behār* 78:142, from *Tohof ol-Ūqūl*.
9   *Behār* 4:221; *At-Towhīd*, p. 72.

4. Elaborations on the Proof of Finitude

And finally, Imam Ja'far as-Sādeq has stated that "Anyone who deliberates on the essence or nature (*dhāt*) of God will [be hurled headlong into bottomless] Perdition."[10]

The Criterion of Quantifiability

Any being who is created will necessarily be finite, discrete, bounded; and as such, it will be a being which is capable of being added to or subtracted from. Imam Ali has stated that "Anything that can be conceived of by the mind (*kolla mā qaddarahu 'aqlon*), or for which the mind can recognize similitudes, will be delimited (*mahdūd*)."[11] And Imam Jawād, the Ninth Imam of the Shi'a, states:

> Verily, with the exception of [God] the Unique (*al-Wāhid*), everything is constituted of parts (*motejazzī*), but God the One (or the Unique, the Singular) is neither constituted of parts, nor can He be increased or taken away from. Anything which is constituted of parts or can be increased or taken away from is a created being and [these attributes] are indicative of their being created and of their having a Creator.[12]

In the *Nahj ol-Balāgha*, we read Imam Ali giving the reason for why this is the case: "... because it is necessary for there to be a difference between the Creator and that which is created, and between He Who imposes limits and that unto which limits are imposed."[13]

Thus, it is not logically possible to conceive of a partner or a second or third "Person" (such as the Son or the Holy Ghost) for Almighty God, Who is not constituted of parts or wholes and is not finite or quantifiable (subject to quantity). In a statement which affirms this tenet, Imam Hasan al-Mojtabā, the Second Imam of the Shi'a, states: "Praise be to God who... does not have a bodily form which is constituted of parts (*motejazzī*) [or can be increased or taken away from], and Who does not have various attributes which would

---

10 *Behār* 3:259; *al-Kāfī*, 1:93.

11 *At-Towhīd*, p. 79.

12 *At-Towhīd*, p. 193; *Behār*, 4:182.

13 *Nahj ol-Balāgha*, p. 40.

[thereby] delimit Him."[14] In other words, a person cannot be God, for a person has a body, which is a form which is limited in space and in time; and as God has no such limitations, to hold that He is a person contravenes the laws of simple logic.

Imam Rezā, the Eighth Imam of the Shi'a, speaks about God in the following apophatic terms:

> ... And anyone who asks concerning the time in which He came into being, has conceived of Him in terms of His being contained (or containable) in time; and anyone who asks concerning His location, has conceived of His essence as being capable of being delimited in space; and anyone who seeks the limits of His being has conceived of Him as being discrete and capable of limitation and enumeration; and anyone who considers Him as being finite and delimited, has conceived of Him as having modules or constituent parts; and anyone who considers Him as having modules or constituent parts, has conceived of Him as being describable; and anyone who considers Him to be describable, has become an unbeliever (*molhad*).[15]

Thus, the proper juxtaposition of the nature of the Creator and that of created beings is the juxtaposition of that which is not quantifiable with that which is quantifiable. The qualitative difference between the nature of the beings of the Creator and that which is created should not be juxtaposed on the basis of the former's (the Creator's) being infinite in terms of time and space, and that of created beings having been endowed with a fraction or some given portion of that *same* reality. Rather, the juxtaposition of the essence of the beings of the Creator and that of created beings should be based on the fact that created beings have the attribute of quantity or measure or number or that which is discrete and quantifiable within a specific given time and space (all of which are necessarily limited and finite); whereas the essence of the sublimely transcendent Creator is exalted far above being able to be described as being a part or a whole, or having quantity or measure or number, and is sublimely exalted above that which is discrete and thus quantifiable within a specific

---

14 *Behār* 4:298; *At-Towhīd*, p. 45.
15 *Ūyūn Akhbār ar-Rezā*, 1:124.

4. Elaborations on the Proof of Finitude

given time and space, as was, for example, the Christ Jesus, the son of the Virgin Lady Mary. The attributes of that which is created is specific to them and pertains exclusively to them: time and space, extension and measure, quantity and number, numerical finitude or lack thereof, being within or without, being born and coming into being, manifestations and epiphanies, heterogeneity, variegation and multiplicity, abundance and privation, parts and wholes – all these are attributes of created beings who have extension and are quantifiable in terms of measure and number.

Any Possible Being must Necessarily have a Creator

Any being whose existence is possible and not necessary or impossible must necessarily have a creator as it is not possible for such a being to come into being on its own. In *Sūrat at-Tūr*, Almighty God poses the following rhetorical question to the atheists:

أَمْ خُلِقُوا مِنْ غَيْرِ شَيْءٍ أَمْ هُمُ الْخَالِقُونَ

> [52:35] [Do they deny the existence of God?] Have they themselves been created without anything [that might have caused their creation]? Or were they, perchance, their own creators?

The question is rhetorical, as Imam as-Sādeq explains with another question: "How is it possible for nothing to create something!?"[16] And elsewhere he tells us: "You yourself know that "nothingness" or "non-being" (*ma'dūm*) does not create anything."[17] In other words, the answer is that it is obvious and, as such, does not stand in need of explanation.

The essence of anything is known by way of that which is its cause; therefore any essence (i.e. the essence of anything) which can be understood in terms of its origin and causation cannot by this definition be a deity worthy of worship; as it is not the Creator but is itself created. God cannot be known or does not disclose Himself to anyone by way of reasons or causes of His origin and causation, as He is unoriginated and uncaused. Nor can anything which can obtain in

---

16   *Behār* 3:158.

17   *Behār* 3:538; *At-Towhīd*, p. 290.

time and space be thought of as being God as this would limit God's infinitude in the finitude of a given location in space and time.

Imam Mohammad al-Bāqer, the Fifth Imam of the Shi'a, tells us that "Verily, God, the Sublimely Exalted, manifests His Providential Lordship (*rububīat*) through His act of creation."[18] In a forceful framing of the question, Imam Rezā continues in the same vein: "How is one who does not balk at his being created himself (*man lā yamtani' min al-inshā'*) [then able] to create anything?" The Imam then goes on to explain:

> "A creature concerning whose being creation is possible and whose being has the ontic capacity of being created (or of coming into being) is thereby branded with an indicator of being an artifice (*āya' al-masnū'*) [in the archaic sense of being something that is created by an artificer]; and rather than [being positioned in a situation where the fact of] his being is indicated [by virtue of the effects of his creative genius], he himself would, rather, become a reason and indicator of the existence of another [One, Who is *his* Creator]."[19]

The Singularity and Dualist Ontology

Imam Ja'far as-Sādeq states concerning the two species of being: "Verily, God is [ontologically and qualitatively] separate from His creation, and His creation is [ontologically and qualitatively] separate from Him."[20] In a similar vein, Imam al-Kāzem, the seventh Imam of the Shi'a, states that "Only God is *qadīm* (eternal; prior to the creation of time), and other than Him, all things are created; and He is far exalted above having the attributes of [any of] His creation."[21] Addressing the monists (i.e. those who believe that there is only one ontological reality, and that God is part and parcel of His creation and is identical with it – the position of the pantheists and theosophers like Eben'Arabī and Mollā Sadra who believe in the theory of the unicity of being or *whadat al-wujud*), Imam Rezā states: "If the situation was

---

18 *Behār* 3:224.

19 *At-Towhīd*, p. 40.

20 *Behār* 4:149; *At-Towhīd* p. 105; *al-Kāfī* 1:83.

21 *At-Towhīd* p. 76; *Behār* 4:296.

4. Elaborations on the Proof of Finitude

as they believe, there would be no [qualitative ontological] difference between the Creator and that which is created, and there would be no difference between the originator and that which issues forth from Him; whereas God is the Originator and Creator and there is a difference between Him and the objects of His creation to which He has given form, because there is nothing like unto Him, just as He too is not like anything else."[22] We read elsewhere of Imam Rezā continuing his explication in the same vein concerning the dual nature of the ontological reality of creation and the Creator:

> Thus, anyone who believes that the objects within the world of creation are eternal and timeless [in the sense that God is such] has not understood God to be unique, without pier, and *qadīm* (uncreated, eternal and prior to time)... The Christians say concerning the Messiah (i.e. Christ Jesus, the son of Lady Mary) that his spirit is a part of God and will return to Him, and the Magians also believe that fire and the sun are a part of God and will return to Him. [But] our Lord and Cherisher and Sustainer (*rabb*) is sublimely exalted above being subdivided [into parts] and is above alterations in His condition [which is unchanging]... Woe unto you! How do you allow yourself to have the impertinence and temerity to consider your Lord to be characterized by changes from one state to another, and to ascribe to Him attributes which apply to the creatures of His creation! Sublimely exalted is He above all that you might ascribe to Him! Neither is He subject to change, like creatures who deteriorate and decay, nor does he change [His state] like creatures who are subject to alteration and transmutation.[23]

The Fallacy of "Pre-Eternity" and "Post-Eternity"

The spirit of the Christ, like the spirit of ordinary people, and like the spirit of the Prophet and of the Imams, was created in time. And although these and the spirits of the true believers will continue endlessly in Heaven, this continuance of theirs does not make these spirits eternal in the sense that God is eternal, which is a sense of being prior to the creation of time itself, of being eternal and

---

22 *At-Towhīd* p. 185; *Behār* 4:173; *Oyūn Akhbār ar-Rezā* 1:127.
23 *Behār* 10:344; *al-Ehtejāj*, pages 405 – 408.

uncreated; because the "eternality" of these spirits is pegged on one end to the time of their creation by God, and thus, while they will live endlessly in everlasting Heaven, they are still created beings and not "prior" and uncreated (*qadīm*). Thus, by rights, created beings who will live forever in Heaven should not be called eternal, but should more properly and more specifically be called endless. Islamic metaphysics, being the beneficiary of the divine wisdom of the Imams through their *hadīth* report corpus, distinguishes between *azalic* and *abadic* forms of endlessness. These two words are usually translated respectively as "pre-eternal" and "post-eternal". But this is absurd. Nothing can be pre-eternal, nor can anything be post-eternal. Moslem metaphysicians use the different terms to describe two distinct states which share the attribute of endlessness. The first, *azalī* (or *azalic* to use the English suffix) is used to refer to that which is eternal, i.e. as that which not only has no *end*, but which has no *beginning* either. This is the singularity which we refer to as God, whose proper name is Allāh, based on His Quranic self-disclosure. The second, *abadī* or *abadic* is used to refer to that which *is by no means* eternal, but is a created being or entity which has a beginning in time (the time of its creation), but which is contingently endless, and will continue not "eternally" but endlessly *in time*, like the souls of God's devotees, which will continue endlessly in time as time-bound created entities, in accordance with His will and promise. As this might be a concept that is somewhat alien to many of you, we shall provide a brief list of *abadic* or endless created beings and entities which are contrasted with the one and only singularity which is eternal, i.e. God. The list includes: (1) Heaven and Hell, which are created by God in time, and which have extension, and which extend endlessly from their point of creation in time but are not eternal; (2) angles (ditto); (3) numbers and all abstract thought, and anything else which issues from the minds of created beings, including their minds themselves, of course; (4) the "everlasting" spirits of men and the jinn; (5) the spirit of Jesus; (6) *et cetera*.

In sum, we can say that everything other than God has a nature which is finite and discrete and hence capable of enumeration, and one which has constituent parts and has extension such that it can be described and is quantifiable in terms of measure and number, and which must necessarily be limited in time and in space; and that this class of being has come into being as a result of being created by a Creator Whose nature is utterly different to all of the attributes of His

4. Elaborations on the Proof of Finitude

creation, and Whose essence and nature are sublimely exalted above the categories of parts and wholes, and measure and number, and time and space, and being and non-being, and of timelessness, eternity and endlessness (*abadīat*) and any and all other concepts and states which we care to mention. He created all of these concepts and categories, as well as everything in Creation, all of which creatures depend on His will for their continued existence and sustenance.

The Incarnation

"If, said he, the Father begat the Son, he that was begotten [must have] had a beginning of existence; hence it is clear that there was [a time] when the son was not." — Arius

"Arius held that Christ... was a created being; he was made like other creatures out of nothing... The Son, he argued, had a beginning, while God was without beginning." — John B. Noss in *Man's Religions,* 1968.

"The heathen believe in many gods. Arius thought that to believe that the Son is God as well as that the Father is God would mean that there are two Gods, and that therefore the Christians would be falling back into heathenism." — B. K. Kuiper, *The Church in History,* 1964.

The *Stanford Encyclopedia of Philosophy* tells us that, according to Kierkegaard, "Christian dogma embodies "paradoxes" which are offensive to reason. The central "paradox" is the assertion that the eternal, infinite, transcendent God simultaneously became incarnated as a temporal, finite, human being (Jesus); [and that] there are two possible attitudes we can adopt to this assertion, viz. we can have faith, or we can take offense. What we cannot do, according to Kierkegaard, is believe by virtue of reason. If we choose [to have] faith [in this absurdity] we must suspend our reason in order to believe in something "higher" than reason. In fact we must believe by virtue of the absurd." I put the word "higher" in quotation marks although the quotes were missing in the original, because obviously, abandoning reason for something that is absurd is not and cannot ever be an act of transcendence. I did the same with the word "paradox" because a paradox is something that is not reconcilable with reason, whereas the belief that "the eternal, infinite, transcendent God simultaneously became incarnated as a temporal, finite, human being" is not an assertion which reason cannot resolve. It can resolve it very simply, because it is a simple contradiction of the law of identity. Either something is finite of it is infinite, and it cannot be both at one and the same time without violating the most basic rule of logic. To characterize it as a "paradox", as does Kierkegaard and as have done many Christians before him, then, betrays an inadequate understanding of the very first rule of logic. But let us not single out *pobre* Søren, who is merely the culmination and aggrieved victim of a whole absurdist tradition which includes the famous line of Tertullian's, who said "I believe because it is absurd"; and which goes back to the Gospel of John and to the Council of Nicea of 325 which said that "Jesus Christ is God," the Council of Constantinople of 381 which said that "the Holy Spirit is God," the Council of Ephesus of 431 which said that "human beings are totally depraved," and the Absurdfest of Chalcedon of 451 which said that "Jesus Christ is both ["totally depraved"] man and God." I guess that made the most sense, so it stuck.

A being who is finite and discrete and hence capable of enumeration, and one which has constituent parts and has extension such that it can be described in terms of measure and number, must necessarily be limited in time and in space. And in addition to the fact that such a being which is capable of being created and of being annihilated itself necessarily stands in need of having a creator (as we saw above), it also follows that such a being can never create a being who is "prior" or eternal (*azalic*) i.e. who is uncreated (*qadīm*), for this would be tautological or a case of putting the cart before the horse.

In another passage which can be used as a refutation of the Christian concept of the trinity with reliance on the unicity of God, Imam Ja'far as-Sādeq tells us that "If there was a being in eternity with God, it would not be possible for God to be the creator of this being, as this being would always have been with God, such that [the unanswerable question would arise as to] how it would be possible for God to create something which was eternally [co-equal] with Him?!"

In a passage which stands out as being a tailor made refutation of the Christian belief in the incarnation of God in the Christ, Imam Ali states, addressing God: "You are not of the same substance or similar to various and sundry phenomena and objects, so that consequently

4. Elaborations on the Proof of Finitude

the truth of Your essence would be manifest, and [thus] understood [thereby]."[24]

The Incarnation through the Lens of John Hick

The philosopher and theologian John Harwood Hick who Robert Smid states "is regularly cited as 'one of the most – if not simply the most – significant philosopher of religion in the twentieth century'"[25] delivered a lecture in Tehran in March of 2005. I will quote the lecture at length, not so much as a buttress of my earlier argument against the logically absurd position of the Christ Jesus son of Lady Mary being "fully God and fully man at one and the same time" – that argument, which is based on the proof of man and God's natures being two distinct and different things, does not stand in need of buttressing. Rather, I thought it worthwhile to allocate some space to this exposition for the purposes of showing how Christianity unravels *itself* as a symptom of what is called post-modernity, and as a symptom of what we believe to be the end times. Thus, it is included not so much as a critique of Christianity (which it undeniably is), as much as an indication of how the collapse of the *grand récit* (Lyotard) of Christianity has taken place at the hands of Christianity itself. So let us attempt to approach Professor Hick's words in a spirit that is cognizant of the fact that the same Ouroboros serpent who is metaphorically prophesied to make its appearance in the End Times, is busy eating its tail in the Sunni and Shi'a traditions with an ineluctable appetite that is just as voracious. Hick tells us concerning the doctrine of the incarnation that,

> It is now widely agreed among New Testament scholars that Jesus himself, the historical individual, did not think of himself as divine and did not teach anything like the later doctrine of the Incarnation. The New Testament sayings in which Jesus seems to claim divinity, such as 'He who has seen me has seen the Father', 'I and the Father are one', 'I am the way, the truth, and the life; no one comes to the Father but by me', are all in the fourth gospel, the gospel of John, and it is widely agreed that they cannot responsibly be attributed to the historical Jesus, but are

---

24 *Behār* 95:254, taken from mahj od-Da'wāt.
25 Smid, Robert (1998–1999). "John Harwood Hick". *Boston Collaborative Encyclopedia of Western Theology*.

words put into his mouth by a Christian writer around the end of the first century, some seventy or so years after Jesus' time, and expressing the developing faith of the church at that time.

So far, we have it from a highly authoritative Christian biblical scholar that it is "widely agreed among New Testament scholars" that "Jesus did not think of himself as divine and did not teach anything like the later doctrine of the Incarnation." Yet, this fact is not headline news or is not a news item that is quite ready for prime-time, and so the belief persists. But wait; it gets even more bizarre. Hick proceeds to quote a representative sample of a few contemporary Christian biblical scholars who are "all personally firm believers in the orthodox doctrine of the Incarnation", but who nevertheless do not believe that the doctrine was taught by Jesus himself.

Referring to the fourth gospel sayings which I have just cited, the doyen of conservative New Testament scholars in Britain, Professor Charles Moule of Cambridge University, wrote, 'Any case for a 'high' Christology [that is, one affirming Jesus' divinity] that depended on the authenticity of the alleged claims of Jesus about himself, especially in the Fourth Gospel, would indeed be precarious' (*The Origin of Christology*, 1977, 136). Then, a former Archbishop of Canterbury, Michael Ramsey, who was also a distinguished New Testament scholar, wrote quite bluntly, 'Jesus did not claim deity for himself' (*Jesus and the Living Past*, 1980, 39). And one of the leading generally conservative British New Testament scholars today, Professor James Dunn of Durham University, says that 'there was no real evidence in the earliest Jesus tradition of what could fairly be called a consciousness of divinity' (*Christology in the Making*, 1980, 60).

Hick concludes: "Indeed in the earliest gospel, that of Mark, Jesus is reported as saying, 'Why do you call me good? No one is good but God alone' (Mark 10: 18)."

Is this utterly bizarre only to my mind? The latest and greatest scientific and historical thinking on the issue of the incarnation espoused by such luminaries as Professor Charles Moule of Cambridge University, the doyen of conservative New Testament scholars in Britain, and Michael Ramsey, a former Archbishop of Canterbury, maintain that 'Jesus did not claim deity for himself'; yet not only the Pope and the common folk continue to hold onto the belief (due to some institutional inertia

4. Elaborations on the Proof of Finitude

or whatnot), but they *themselves* continue to believe it! Presumably, they can make a better case for "a 'high' Christology" than the Christ himself as "revelation [being] necessarily mediated through human beings in all their specific historical particularity" (John Hick), they are in a better position than God Himself to judge these things, having a higher historical perspective and all.

It gets curiouser and curiouser[26] when we continue to read Hick talking about the issue of Jesus being the "Son of God". Here he states that in Judaism any outstandingly pious Jew could be called a son of God which was meant as someone who was close to God or one who was doing God's will, and that within Judaism this usage was obviously metaphorical. Hick states that Jesus himself used the expression metaphorically when he said that we are to forgive our enemies 'so that you may be sons of your father who is in heaven' (Matthew 5: 45), and again in the Lord's Prayer where he taught that we were to address God as 'Our Father who is in heaven'. But then what happened, in the period between Jesus' lifetime and the full development of the trinitarian doctrine, is that the *metaphorical* son of God was transformed in Christian thinking into the *metaphysical* God the Son, second person of a divine trinity.

And so, consequently, a division soon began within the very early church between the original Jewish Christianity based in Jerusalem, which continued for a while as a new movement within Judaism, seeing Jesus as a human being with a special divine calling, and on the other hand the Pauline development which took the Jesus movement far beyond Judaism into the Hellenistic world and exalted Jesus to a divine status.

And here comes the *coup de grâce* of John Hick's lecture *Islam and Christianity*, which he was kind enough to deliver to the Iranian Institute of Philosophy, under the auspices of the Iranian Institute for Interreligious Dialogue, in Tehran in the March of 2005, and put us all out of our misery. He tells us that his own understanding of Jesus as a human being rather than as God incarnate differs from the Quranic understanding of him only at two points, the first of which

---

26 Forgive me, for, like Alice, I was so much surprised, that for the moment I quite forgot how to speak good English.

is the immaculate conception of the Christ Jesus by Lady Mary. Here Professor Hick quotes 2:47 of the Quran as well as Matt. 1: 18 and Luke 1: 25 where the story of the Immaculate Conception is "similar[ly]" stated. But then he says that:

> However in the New Testament as a whole the story has a very slender basis, occurring only in these two relatively late Gospels, eighty or more years after the event, and seems to be unknown to all the other, mostly earlier, New Testament writers. For this reason, together with the fact that miraculous birth stories tended to gather around great figures in the ancient world – for example, the Buddha, Zoroaster, and various figures in Greek and Roman religion - many New Testament scholars today doubt its historicity. Following them I myself do not affirm the virginal conception of Jesus.

So help me out here. Have I understood rightly that "the most significant [theologian and] philosopher of religion of the twentieth century" is saying that the Christ Jesus (unto whom be God's peace) *was* God, despite the fact that "It is now widely agreed among New Testament scholars that Jesus himself, the historical individual, did not think of himself as divine and did not teach anything like the later doctrine of the Incarnation"; and that furthermore, – wait for it! – and also in direct contradiction of what the Bible states, he believes that Jesus was *not* conceived of immaculately, but that his was an ignominious out of wedlock birth? Or is it just *my* bastardly interpretation of what Hick is actually saying??

(The other point at which he differs from the Quranic account of Jesus is on the issue of the crucifixion, which, contra the Quran, Hicks believes did in fact take place.)

And so to conclude this section; to our mind, this state of affairs is the philosophical equivalent of slurring one's words like a drunk, and degenerating into babble. It makes no sense to say that the Christ did not claim deity for himself, but that I choose to ascribe that to him anyway. It is the height of absurdity. And the other thing is beyond absurd and downright insulting. God forbid that we should ascribe such ignominy to Lady Mary, the mother of Jesus (unto both of whom be God's peace and blessings). And make no mistake: the moral slouching to Gomorrah

4. Elaborations on the Proof of Finitude

is necessarily preceded by this kind of intellectual sloth and fuzziness. Here is an example from that darling of latter day Protestants and existentialists, the absurdist Soren Kierkegaard: "The absurdity of atonement requires faith that we believe that for God even the impossible is possible, including the forgiveness of the unforgivable."[27] Absurdity is here used in a positive sense; the impossible is equated with its opposite, the possible, and forgiveness is equated with its opposite, the unforgivable. Nonsense, in other words; a veritable latter day Tower of Babble. And of course Kierkegaard has his ancient antecedents in the likes of the famous lines from Tertullian: "I believe because it is absurd," which is based on the idea that reason alone is insufficient. And while that is true enough, and it is certainly true that reason stands in need of revelation, what has happened in the Christian tradition is that rather than scripture transcending *above* reason and being a faculty that is trans- or supra-rational (and thus fully in line with the demands of reason), religion became something that was at odds with reason and hence became irrational.

---

27 Quoted in the *Stanford Encyclopedia of Philosophy.*

5. *al-Haqq* and the Referential Theory of Knowledge

In the chapters that follow, we shall critique the philosophical approach as method, as well as discuss a critique of the methodological bases of Christianity and the thought of Dugin and de Benoist, and of the substantive issues of all three of these ideologies which have arisen out of this flawed method. Beside the substantive critique of Christianity which we have already discussed (mainly with regards to the incarnation), the rest of the book deals with a substantive critique of the thought of Dugin and de Benoist, which is based on that of Heidegger and Nietzsche, all four of whom share the error of a subjectivist epistemology and a pluralist ontology (and thus of being anti-foundationalist). This is a trend that they started at their time, whose epistemological zeitgeist can be characterized as being a flawed continuation and exacerbation of the epistemological error of the Enlightenment thinkers, where, generally speaking, Descartes, Spinoza and Leibniz limited that which was considered to be "scientific" to the domain of the rational; and where Bacon, Locke and Newton confined that truth which properly represented reality to the domain of that which could be verified empirically. Both of these epistemic postures were self-imposed straight-jackets which were donned in an attempt to jettison the superstitions of tradition, which were mainly rooted in Christian revelation. Kant came up with his neumenon/ phenomenon distinction in order to try to save revelation, but he turned everything inside out by doing so, so that the philosophers who followed him, the greatest of whom were Kierkegaard, Nietzsche and Heidegger, following the pied piper Kant, went further than the rationalists and empiricists, and rejected the possibility of any sort of correspondence of truth with reality (hence the rejection of any correspondence theory of truth, and hence the rejection of the possibility of any foundation for such correspondence – as the neumenon was posited as being out of reach). This chapter deals with the ontological aspects of this issue. Chapter 14 (Objective Truth and Radical Postmodern Subjectivism, and especially its culmination, "Extra Ecclesiam nulla Salus and its Alternative: the Zombification of the Soul") deal with the epistemological aspects of it, and we end the book with Chapter 15 (Spiritual Affinity and the Principle of Avowal and Disavowal), which in part illustrates the fallacy of non-foundational paradigms by providing some practical examples of the flaws of non-foundationalist thinking.

* * *

It is important to fully understand the ontological bifurcation between the nature of God and the nature of the created world before we proceed further. On the ultimate level, there is only one reality, only one reality which is truly real, and that is the reality of that species of being which we refer to as God, Who is, as we just stated, the One (*al-Ahad*), i.e., Who is the only One who is Eternally Self-Sufficient and Absolute (*as-Samad*). And on a lower level, because He is Most Gracious and Beneficent, He has created creation, which constitutes this second order of reality, which is dependent on Him for every aspect of its being, and whose being thus takes on a second-tier order of reality. Now within this second-tier reality of God's creation, which is what the Quran refers to as the *donyā* or the Lower World, there are creatures which have been given a limited amount of free will; that is, we human beings. And because the world of creation is based on a Divine Order, and because this order is a moral order, the order or reality of us denizens of this Lower World (or the extent and magnitude of our reality, of our ontic amplitude) depends on the moral value of each of our individual lives, on the extent to which we decide to conform our lives with that which is *ultimately* (and not secondarily) real; on the extent to which we decide to conform our will to that of God's. If we define Islam as one's self-surrender to the will of God, then the extent to which we are real is comensureate with the extent of our Islam, our piety and righteousness within the rank of those who have submitted themselves to God's Way and to His religion.

This Way is God's nature, just as Goodness and Justice are God's nature, and both of these are completely infused in the world of His creation. And because He is the only Being Who is self-sufficient and eternal, it is only those attributes which conform to His nature which will survive the test of time and be sustained in perpetuity, because it is only they which share in God's Being, and thus will share in His attribute of Eternality, albeit contingently. This attribute of God's is called *al-haqq*, that which is real, true, just, good, and everlasting. The opposite of *al-haqq* is everything that is not real, true, just, good, and is thus doomed to perish in time. That is why God says that now

5. al-Haqq and the Referential Theory of Knowledge

that *al-haqq* has now come to light (by way of the Quranic revelation), its ontic opposite, *al-bātel,* will consequently and necessarily wither away in the long term (i.e. after the Day of Judgment):

> [17:81] And say: "*al-haqq* has now come [to light], and *al-bātel* has [consequently] withered away: for, behold, [by its very nature] *al-bātel* is bound to perish!"

The two key words of this revelation (*āya*), *al-haqq* and *al-bātel* are invariably translated respectively as "truth" and "falsehood", thus:

> [17:81] And say: "The truth has now come [to light], and falsehood has [consequently] withered away: for, behold, [by its nature] all falsehood is bound to perish!"

These translators err because they do not recognize the fact that the word *al-haqq* represents God, and as such, must represent the ontological conception of God that is present in the Quran, which they fail to do, because the semantic field of the word "truth" is not sufficient to the task as it does not touch upon God's unicity, self-sufficiency and absoluteness, all of which facets reside and are present in the word *al-haqq*. Thus, all of these translations are misleading insofar as truth is only one facet of the key Quranic term *al-haqq*, which is Quranically juxtaposed not just against falsehood, but also, and more importantly, against that which is essentially temporal and, as such, has an expiration date and is therefore not fully real. The Quran also juxtaposes *al-haqq* with that which is untrue and unjust. Thus, *al-haqq* is a key Quranic term which refers to that which is real, just and true; in other words, it refers to those elements within creation which have ontological independence and are therefore everlasting because they exist in God, Who is the only Being Who is self-sufficient and Who is uncreated, and Who is the only Being Who is truly real. The being of everything in creation depends on Him and on the nature of His being. Thus, the above revelation (*āya*) refers not only to a truth value or a value indicating the relation of a proposition to truth; but it is also a statement and a proposition which refers first and foremost to the *ontological or existential value* of its subject.

This concept, the distinction between *al-haqq* and *al-bātel*, is most basic to the proper framing of our argument, so let us bring a couple of other āyas (units of Quranic revelation) to bear on the subject before we proceed further:

> [21:18] Nay, but [by the very act of creation] We hurl *al-haqq* [that which is real] against *al-bātel*, and it crushes the latter: and lo! It withers away. But woe unto you for all your [ill-gotten attempts at] defining [*al-haqq*, i.e. that which is real and is ontologically independent, i.e. God, as something other than God] – [for all such attempts are bound to fail insofar as and to the extent that they are at variance with *al-haqq* or with that which is real, true, just.]

And:

> [34:49] Say: "*al-haqq* has now come [to light], and *al-bātel* is [thus] bound to wither away]: for, *al-bātel* (the absence of reality) cannot bring forth anything new, nor can it bring back [that which has passed away]."

What we see here in the Quran is that God is making a distinction between *al-haqq* and *al-bātel*, and the argument that He proffers to us in the continuation of the second *āya* we quoted above is that not only is there only one reality, but that there can only *be* one reality, as, logically, if there were more than one reality, order could not obtain and there would only be chaos:

> [21:21] And yet some people choose to worship certain earthly things or beings as deities that [are supposed to] resurrect [the dead; and they fail to realize that], [21:22] had there been in heaven or on earth any deities other than God, both [those realms] would of a certainty have fallen into chaos! But limitless in His glory is God, enthroned [in His awesome almightiness and transcendence far] above anything that men may devise by way of definition concerning His reality]!

Toshihiko Izutsu makes the distinction as follows in his *God and Man in the Quran*: "*bātil* (false) as opposed to *haqq* (real)". William Chittick juxtaposes *al-haqq* with *bātil* which he defines as "unreal, vain, null, void". But he elaborates on the concept of *al-haqq* as follows:

5. al-Haqq and the Referential Theory of Knowledge

As a divine name, *al-haqq* means the Real, the Truth, the Right, and it is typically juxtaposed with *khalq*, creation. But everything has a *haqq* pertaining to it, which is to say that everything has a proper situation, a correct mode of being, an appropriate manner of displaying the Real to us. The sense of appropriateness and rightness in *haqq* is very strong, and the words "real" or "truth" simply do not express it in English. To say that everything has a *haqq* is to say that everything has a right and appropriate mode of being and that, in addition, it is our duty before God, the Real, to recognize it and to act accordingly... Each thing has a right upon us, and hence each is our "responsibility" (another word that can translate *haqq*)."

That is alright as far as it goes, but in the above passage, Chittick emphasizes the element of being right and thus of being just: of man's submission and conformity of his free will to God's intended order in creation. And Henry Corbin adds that *al-haqq* refers to the Necessary Being or the Prime Being (*al-haqq al-awwal*). But all of these miss the most important distinction which is that *al-haqq* is *that which resides in God* and is a part of His essence, and as such, is ontologically independent and absolute, and therefore, *eternal*. Thus, God makes the distinction between Being and Time, and tells us that, that which exists as a part of Him in the order of His creation will outlast time and will abide forever, and that which does not conform itself to that which is real and everlasting will, by definition, perish. Given free will, if one commits *kofr* (unbelief, ingratitude, *haqq*-concealing), *zolm* (wrong-doing), and *fesq* (moral corruption), and does not self-surrender his or herself to God's will and to the plan and way of life which He has in mind for us, then he or she will have chosen a path which leads to his or her annihilation in the long term or in the hereafter, once the veil of death is lifted,[1] as it is only righteous behavior that is eternal, as God is righteous and does not abide *kofr*, *zolm* and *fesq* in the least.

OK, so now that we have explicated that only God is real in the true sense of His being the only Being Who is Eternally Self-Sufficient and

---

1   [50:19] And [then,] the stupor of death brings with it [the lifting of the veil which will then expose] the [full] truth of that [very thing, O man,] from which thou wouldst always turn away!

Absolute (*as-Samad*) (see the three-fold proof above in the chapter of Finitude), and that anything that exists but is *not* eternally self-sufficient and absolute (i.e., that exists as a second-tier order of reality) owes its existence to God; we are presently in a position to state it in the following terms: every species of being that exists in the finite, created order of being owes its reality to that other, higher order of reality which is infinite and eternal and self-sufficient and absolute, and which we refer to as God (and Whose proper name is Allāh). Therefore, the reality of every species of being that is finite and created and thus exists in time can only properly be understood and contextualized *with reference to* that other, superior and ultimate species of being. This is an inescapable fact, and it is this reality upon which Plato's referential theory of truth rests. And so, when Alexander Dugin states that:

> Something went wrong at the very beginning of Western history, and Martin Heidegger sees this wrong turn precisely in the affirmation of the exclusivist position of an exclusivist logos. This shift was made by Heraclitus and Parmenides, but above all by Plato with the development of philosophic thought that envisaged two worlds or layers of reality where existence was perceived as the manifestation of the hidden.

Then what we have to say to this is that it is not that Plato "envisaged two worlds or layers of reality"; rather, the unassailable logic of the Proof of Finitude (see above) means that there can be no escape from the fact that there are two tiers to reality. Call it a bi-cameral monism, if you will; one of whose chambers is time and everything that is created and contained within it, and the other "chamber" is not a chamber at all as it does not "contain" anything, as the nature of that substance is infinite and thus is uncontainable, unconceptualizable, unenglishable in its ultimate essence. We do not mean to imply a validation of the Platonic theory of the Forms here or of the Platonic theory of anamnesis, but there can be no question that there are two kinds of reality, one absolute and ultimately real, and the other one conditional and ultimately unreal or one whose reality is dependent on the reality of the Ultimate Reality. And the yardstick for measuring the pilgrim's progress is the degree to which he or she is able to draw nearer to this Ultimate Reality, whose veils or higher levels of reality (*samāwāt*) are gradually and systematically lifted in a process of "the manifestation of the hidden" that is the pilgrim's journey of education

5. al-Haqq and the Referential Theory of Knowledge

and awakening to God. Immediately in the same passage, Alexander Dugin goes on to state that:

> Later, this hidden element was recognized as logos, as the idea, the paradigm, the example. From that point on, the referential theory of truth proceeds. Truth lies in the fact of the immediate correspondence of the given to the presumed invisible essence.

We would say that this is an inescapable logical conclusion, except that we would substitute "correspondence of the given to the presumed invisible essence" with "correspondence of the given to God or to God's essence or God's eternal infinitude."

Thus, we would say that it is not so much a case of being "confused by the nuances of the complicated relationship between Being and thought, between pure Being (*Seyn*) and its expression in existence — a being (*Seiende*), between the human experience of being-in-the-world (*Dasein* — being-there) and being-in-itself (*Sein*)"; in other words, a case of the confusion between Being and [being in] Time, as it is a case of the confusion of Being and Nothingness. Either one conforms his or her conditional being to that of the Being of the Eternally Self-Sufficient and Absolute while he or she is still in time i.e. while there is still time before Judgment Day; or, his or her conditional being will ineluctably wither away into Nothingness upon his or her death or upon having paid for one's sins, having been brought back to life by God to stand in God's judgment. The rise of alienation, 'calculating thinking' (*das rechnende Denken*) and the development of technology to try to compensate for the sense of alienation, and the whole edifice that Heidegger sums up as nihilism did not come about as a result of stating that there is a distance between man's nature (which is conditional) and that which is truly existent and absolutely real, and then to posit that real truth lies in the correspondence of the latter with the former — the referential theory of knowledge. To the contrary, we assert that to the extent that Plato's thought conforms to the above, he was taught or inspired by a prophet, or was influenced by a strain of thought which had a divine origin. Rather, alienation and nihilism can only arise from one source: the failure to abide by God's will, as it has been expressed to mankind through the ages by His prophets, the last of whom was the Most Noble Prophet Mohammad, may God's peace be unto him and unto the Members of his Purified and Immaculate Family.

* * *

We shall now deal briefly with the methodological error that the grafting of Christianity onto Western philosophy by the early Church Fathers, and Augustine and Aquinas and the scholastics represents.

6. Philosophical Ding-Dong at the Mad Hatter's Tea Party

What has brought on what we think of as the crisis of modernity in the West is a social and cultural context of increasing doubt about a religion whose ability to deliver reliable knowledge about God and the world decreases in direct proportion to the developments in the natural sciences and in the science of historiography, all of which have undermined positions that were developed on the basis of fallible human philosophical methods rather than on firm revelational footings, and so the Magisterium became untenable as a result of the changes in human knowledge brought about by the scientific revolution and everything that followed in its wake. The central philosophical allegation against 'the modernists' was that they had displaced Aristotle with Kant; in the thirteenth century, it was those who displaced Plato with Aristotle, thus radically changing Augustinian Christianity.1 And so on. Anthony Carrol gets it right when he places the problem of modernity in the larger philosophical context, and reminds us of Nominalism as one of the early precursor cracks which adumbrated the deluge to come, characterizing "modernity" as a straw man set up against the deeper problems facing the Church:

> [Pope St. Pius X's Encyclical against modernism,] *Pascendi*, [issued on September 8, 1907] in many ways constructs modernism as a straw man in order to defend a certain style of philosophy and theology that had been designated as official for the Catholic Church by Pope Leo XIII in his 1879 Encyclical *Aeterni Patris*: that of Saint Thomas Aquinas... However, the roots of what is termed 'philosophical modernism' lie well before the modernist crisis of the twentieth century. In fact, one has to trace them back to the break-up of the medieval synthesis in theology and philosophy that was ushered in by Nominalism in the eleventh century. Nominalism was a philosophical movement that held that it was not possible to know universals or general realities, but that all one could safely come to know and to talk sensibly about were particulars. The

---
1   Joe Egerton, *Faith, Reason and the Modernists*, 2009.

tendency towards this thought led to a disbelief in a realist approach to the world and so too the view that one could come to know God in and through sensible reality. This breakdown of the medieval synthesis of thought was further intensified by scientific advances which gradually discredited the Aristotelian conception of the universe.[2]

As long as the teaching of the Church is tethered to philosophy and its creedal footing has philosophical rather than revealed bases, the Copernican shift that the Second Vatican Council inaugurated within the Church is justified, because the edifice to which it is tethered went through its own Copernican shift with the changes to the philosophical sensibility brought to it by the likes of Suárez, Descartes, Bacon, Kant, Locke and Hume; because the challenge of developing ways of propagating and defending a "philosophical faith" that are more than simply condemnatory of the modern world, if they can be achieved at all with the objective of attaining to "a coherent philosophical footing", will be achieved through some other philosophical antithesis, which in turn will mature into a synthesis, only to be challenged by a new thesis which will start the whole process over again, and continue *ad infinitum* in a Hegelian dialectical process which puts the whole foundation of how we are to live in an eternal state of tension and chaos – a state of affairs that would make any demiurge or gnostic archon warden proud of his role as Keeper of the World as Crypt with the shards of light busy going around in circles in the Tower of Babel of their own creation.

If not Nominalism or the Kantian madness, it will be some other new-fangled tomfoolery, such as Barth's offering of the *analogia fidei* ("analogy of faith"), that is, the insights of faith based on revelation instead of the Thomist *analogia entis* ("analogy of being"), the upshot of this latest revolution (or the "Barthian captivity," as Reinhold Niebuhr called it) being that all forms of liberalism fell more or less into discredit. And so on *ad infinitum*, playing Philosophical Ding-Dong at the Mad Hatter's Tea Party. The lesson is: philosophy is the quicksilver that revelation was sent down from on high *to preclude humanity from having to touch*, for touch it enough and we will surely become "as mad as a hatter."

---

2   Anthony Carroll, *Modernism: The Philosophical Foundations*, 2009.

6. Philosophical Ding-Dong at the Mad Hatter's Tea Party

"A coherent philosophical footing" is an oxymoron that is bested only by the term "philosophical faith". Philosophy is for those who have failed to attain to the certainty of faith. And so the solution is to recognize the need for a stability whose only basis can be revealed knowledge concerning the world beyond the ken of ordinary human perception. But of course, alas, the Christian tradition is not privy to such revealed information that is sufficiently comprehensive, first of all; and secondly, the information it is privy to is not endowed with a sufficient degree of probative force in the chain of custody of the scriptural text's provenance title (*sanad*) as to pass the test of reason for its veracity.

Make no mistake: the issues of the historicity of Christian scripture which Ferdinand Christian Bauer and his Tübingen School of theology were perhaps the first to take on seriously in the modern era are not going anywhere; nor can any person of goodwill who avers his allegiance to reason ignore the fact that the Gospels are full of internal contradictions, let alone the fact that they contradict each other on important points and are furthermore contradicted by what are uncontestable historical facts. But I digress, and I apologize if I have spoken too frankly; but I do so because I believe I am in the company of friends. Certainly I consider myself to be a friend of traditional Catholicism and of the Catholic as well as the Orthodox Churches (if not a friend of the former's post-Vatican II incarnation).

7. Philosophy as the Continuance of a Pagan Farce

The Western philosophical tradition is nothing less than the continuance of an irrational farce of pagan antiquity. How much longer do we have to go through the ever more intricate and arcane writings of yet another philosopher who does not accept a single assumption of any of his predecessors and forebears? How much longer must we suffer through more complete upheavals in the Western intellectual tradition such as the Copernican Revolution that Kant inflicted on Western thought? How many more swipes of the sword must we suffer through, such as the swipe of Hume's sword, whose radical skepsis cut both legs from under the intellectual body of Western philosophy, after which what was left of its truncated form has been hobbling forward ever since? How many more Nietzsches and Kierkegaards do we have to suffer through, each of which took their hand and wiped all of the pieces of the chessboard of the Western intellectual tradition clean away, saying they don't want to play that game anymore, but want to play a different game; Nietzsche for the atheistic branch and Kierkegaard for the theistic one. And now another contender comes in the form of Martin Heidegger, proclaiming that *phusis* and *logos* and *chaos* and *aletheia* and every other basic concept under the sun is wrong, wrong, wrong! And what is more, it is wrong! (But that the National Socialists nearly got it right, if only they had been a tad more radical.) In short, "What has Athens to do with Jerusalem?" To quote Tertullian in one of his better moments, where he likens philosophy to a form of gnosticism in so far as it maintains that reason alone is sufficient, and correctly sees philosophy as a comprehensive method and world view to be the most serious threat to Christian orthodoxy.

Is this the kind of world we have been "thrown" into? A veritable intellectual Tower of Babel, where chaos reigns supreme and no one understands a word of what the other is saying? Because if you take a step back and take a moment to think about it, that is what philosophy is: from the very beginning of recorded history, going back to the pre-Socratics, the entire output of the "high art and science" of philosophy has produced nothing but a bunch of sophisticated tomes, each offering a different view of what the world is supposedly all about, and all of them, without exception, disagreeing with each other. And this disagreement is not a disagreement on minor details; rather, it is a radical disagreement, to the extent that the great names in the history of philosophy have failed to agree on *a single first principle*!

It is madness! It is insane to think that a world that is created with the exacting craftsmanship that would put a Swiss watchmaker to shame, a world where a single degree change in any of the constants in nature, be it the gravitational force, the strong or weak nuclear forces, the speeds of sound and of light, the speed of the winds, the temperatures of the oceans, the thickness of the ozone layer, the thickness of our skins... need I go on? And of the millions upon millions of constants in the way the world is created – if *any* of these are fiddled with and changed even to a single degree, the whole order of nature will fall apart and everything will be destroyed. And that is exactly what we human beings are doing. We do not listen to the guidance that is sent to us from Above, from our Maker, preferring instead to glory in our arrogance, and to destroy the perfect world that we have been given in trust. It is madness to think that in a world of such exacting craftsmanship, the mind of man and his noosphere would be left to wallow in such chaos for eternity. Is that how little we think of the world of creation and of the sense of balance and harmony of its Maker? Or of His grace and loving kindness towards us, His highest creation?

What kind of god, other than one that would conform to the description which the gnostics gave to the demiurges they believed in, who were the wardens and prison guards of the world which they envisioned to be a crypt – what kind of god would scramble the minds of his subjects to the extent that they would not be able to agree on a single first principle for the entire duration of their intellectual activity? Certainly not a loving god. What kind of god would intentionally change the languages of his subjects so that they would no longer understand each other, and would only babble at each other henceforth. What kind of god would confound the speech of his subjects so that they could no longer understand each other, if not a gnostic turnkey-demiurge? Is it a wonder that Marcion of Sinope rejected the deity described in the Hebrew Scriptures?

This is the basic difference we Moslems have with our Christian cousins to our west; with those who have emigrated away from the

7. Philosophy as the Continuance of a Pagan Farce

heartland of revelation, and have gradually lost the sense that the God who made us also told us what His intention was in His creating us, and told us where we came from, where we are, and where we should and should not be going. It is that simple. It is a basic percept, like the image of the Rubin's vase below:

Sure, one can certainly take the position that there are two shadows of human forms facing each other; but is that really how you want to go through life? Accentuating the negative? God has created us in such a way as to give us a choice; He has created us with free will. But He has also sent His apostles through the ages to tell us what the right way is, and what is the wrong way; what will enable us to attain to felicity in the hereafter and what will ensure our ultimate doom. It's called Humanism: insisting on seeing a human face into everything where one does not really exist. And it is a symptom of modernity.

And when we say that things are really as simple and clear cut as this, we are accused of being "irrational" and "illogical" and "unsophisticated"; or that we are hicks who fall in the category of the kind of people who believe, with the Russian Old Believers, bless their beautiful hearts, in 'the sin of boiled buckwheat' (to use an example from Alexander's book). The fact is that it is all those who believe in philosophy and its efficacy in being able to address the basic issues of the human condition that are unsophisticated and irrational hicks. It is beyond being irrational to continue for 2,500+ years of not achieving the desired result (which is arriving at truth and how best to live one's life) and to expect a different result. They say that the definition of insanity is doing the same thing over and over again and expecting a different result. That is not, strictly speaking, true; but you get the idea. It is madness to continue to try to come up with the solution to the same problem when the solution has been provided by the last of the prophets to be sent to humanity, and has been explicated profusely by the twelve Imams who were divinely commissioned to explain the final message.

It is irrational to try to understand ultimate being, which is infinite, with an instrument the range of whose calipers is finite; namely, the instrument of reason. Concepts are the grist for the mill of the faculty of reason; and concepts are discrete, bounded, finite entities. Otherwise, we would not be able to get our minds around them. But alas, that which the philosophers have been trying for millennia to get their minds around is *not* finite. This is a basic mistake of Heidegger's: he mistakes the human being, who in his or her essence, is an endless spirit that will live on forever *inshā'allāh* (if God wills), insofar as his or her spirit resides in God, with a time-bound, finite entity. And so, what he is trying to do is to drink an endless ocean with a teaspoon.

Our rational faculty of intellection reasons that on one hand, it can see that our being is infinitely complex, or is at least so complex that it cannot "get its mind around it"; and that on the other hand, reason itself operates by the application of discrete (bounded and finite) concepts and categories which it processes in series in order to make sense of things. (There are other ways in which other faculties "make sense" of things, such as intuition, which takes things in, in parallel or as a whole, but the faculty of intuition is subjective or intersubjective at best, and never objective, which is why philosophers reject it as a source of objective understanding, as do the magisters and theosophers of Shi'a Islam). And so, the sound rational faculty of intellection reasons that its ability to understand the world is limited in certain very basic and fundamental ways. Given this correct unassuming and self-effacing posture, reason welcomes true revelation.

From the religious point of view, the mind of the philosopher is in a sense defective because it is unable to see the limitations of the efficacy and compass of reason, and so when it comes across revelation, it rejects it, preferring to cling onto reason even after the nullity of its efficacy has long been established or should have been. Having rejected revelation, it is left only with reason, and so it applies the only tool which it has at its disposal to try to understand existence, which is a tool that by its own admission is too blunt and not suitable for the task. But for the

7. Philosophy as the Continuance of a Pagan Farce

religious person, a sound mind, with its rational faculty operating at its full capacity, sees that reason is limited as a tool for understanding the entirety of existence. Reason is like a spot light, and is highly useful for detailed work in specific areas, but it is not a floodlight, which is what is required. Reason itself, again, when working at its full capacity, sees this, i.e. the limits of its own efficacy. And so, given this, the religious thinker contends, reason recognizes revelation when confronted with it, and welcomes it under certain circumstances such as it being accompanied by the miracles of the apostles and prophets who convey it, and bows down and defers to it in areas where the limits of its own jurisdiction prevent it from treading.

As Brother Alexander himself states, "The 'disenchantment of the world' (Max Weber), and the 'end of the sacred'… was the core of the New Era of modernity: man came to replace God, philosophy and science replaced religion, and the rational, forceful, and technological constructs took the place of revelation." Thus, if we want to roll back the 'disenchantment of the world', God must replace man, religion must replace philosophy and [secular] science, and "the rational, forceful, and technological constructs" must give way to revelation.

But one of the most virulent of problems that the philosophers of the West have is that they think that their minds are more sophisticated than the mind of God, and this is manifested in the sentiment about logos "whose rationalist procedures of thought (logic) are 'an invention of schoolteachers, not philosophers'". I am not sure who to attribute the quote to, Nietzsche or Heidegger, but it does not matter; both have the same holier-than-thou attitude. But the matter is really simple. It comes down to whether one prefers to think of the world of creation as a place that is created by a benevolent Supreme Being Who has made the logic of His Ways in such a manner as to be readily understandable by all of his creation; or to think of creation as being a place that might or might not be created, but in either event is a place that resembles a creation of a gnostic demiurge who is intent on keeping the denizens of his world-as-crypt confused and in the dark, and always at odds with each other with respect to even the most basic of principles, such that as soon as some brilliant philosophical mind comes up with a breakthrough, his or her shining thesis is almost immediately undermined by some other bright spark, so that they are all lined up on each other's shoulders like so many caryatids. Isn't religion supposed to put an end to this madness of constantly spinning around in ever wider circles in search of yet another theory that is destined to be replaced by yet another one. Is *this* the Plan of an All-Wise and All-Merciful creator? The problem is that most philosophers are so drunk on having imbibed the philosophical Kool-Aid that the only way they can answer this question is to stop philosophizing for a while and sober up. It is only then that they will be able to see the question in the true light and in the true context in which it is framed. May God give them the humility to see and accept guidance when it is provided to them. Āmīn.

8. The "Curious Disputations" of Greek Philosophy

Heidegger's cosmology fails to take into account the only thing that is real, namely the vast, endless domain of existence which awaits us in the hereafter. Christianity does a much better job there, but then it too gets all tied up into knots because of its having grafted itself, without any authority from Heaven to do so, on Greek philosophy. And this was Catholicism's fatal error, which landed it in the crises of the Great Schism of circa 1054, in Luther's Revolt of 1517, and ultimately, in the self-inflicted broadside of the Second Vatican Council of 1962-5. And this is because there has not been *a single substantive issue or first principle, even, that philosophers have been able to agree upon throughout all of recorded history* (and this includes, of course, philosophers within the Islamic world as well). In the following *āyas* (revelations), God characterizes this state of affairs as man's being in a state of confusion and "utter darkness" (*az-zolomāt*), out of which only He can lead us, from the darkness of speculation into the light of certainty:

> [51:8] Verily, [O men,] you are deeply at variance as to what to believe: [51:9] perverted in his views thereon is he who would deceive himself! [51:10] They but destroy themselves, they who are given to guessing at what they cannot ascertain – [51:11] they who blunder along, lost in ignorance, [and floundering] heedless in a flood of confusion.

> [57:9] It is He who bestows from on high clear messages [about which you can be certain of] unto [this] His servant, to lead you out of [your] utter darkness into the light: for, behold, God is most compassionate towards you, and a dispenser of grace.

But when E. Michael Jones talks about St. John writing his Gospel in Greek and the consequent grafting of the message of the Christ onto the "Curious Disputations" (Tertullian) of the Greek philosophical tradition, he talks about this fact as if it is a *good* thing. But then he goes on to bemoan the modernist onslaught on the Aristotelian-Thomist edifice of the schoolmen as the official philosophical underpinnings of the Church as if *that* is a *bad* thing. This is a contradiction. Because, surely, the whole modernist onslaught on that system, from Descartes and Kant and Hegel to Locke and Hume, is part and parcel of the critical philosophy which has its roots in and is the heritage of the philosophical tradition of the Greeks. These modern philosophers were the greatest minds Europe had on offer, working away in the methodology that goes back to Anaxagoras and the Pre-Socratics, applying it to the new conditions and data which they observed. Pope Benedict XVI said as much in his Regensburg address of September 2006:

> "A critique of modern reason from within has nothing to do with putting the clock back to the time before the Enlightenment and rejecting the insights of the modern age. The positive aspects of modernity are to be acknowledged unreservedly: we are all grateful for the marvelous possibilities that it has opened up for mankind and for the progress in humanity that has been granted to us."

As Joe Egerton says, "The message of [the] pope is unambiguous: rational enquiry is a good, and that extends to the enquiries of the great modern philosophers."[1] Of course we *also* believe that rational enquiry is a good, but where we differ is on the compass of reason, and that it should be limited and confirmed by revelation. And we assert that this is a rational position (and that the failure to limit reason's compass is irrational – a hyper-rationality or irrationalism that is ultimately self-undermining absent the corrective of revelation, and which thus leads "rational" enquiry either into nihilism or philosophical skepticism or into the solipsistic maze of the subjective idealism that is the hallmark of philosophical and/ or existential religion).

Kant states that Locke "sensualized all concepts of understanding", whereas Descartes had previously "conceptualized sensations". Absent the grounding of the faculty of revelation, there is no way to get off this Merry-go-Round; and so, one who goes down that path and ignores the truths of revelation will get dizzy from too much conceptualization without grounding (like static electricity that builds up without a ground), but rationalizes to himself that he is not dizzy and/or mentally exhausted.

---

1 See Joe Egerton, *Faith, Reason and the Modernists*, 2009.

8. The "Curious Disputations" of Greek Philosophy

Now these philosophers were all wrong, of course. But wait. What am I saying?? Philosophy *itself* is all wrong! Philosophy and speculative (as opposed to creedal or dogmatic) metaphysics and theology are at best the blind man's guesses as to the realities of the world that is beyond the ken of ordinary human perception. As the Quran characterizes such philosophical and theological speculators:

> [30:7] They know but the outer surface of this world's life, whereas of the ultimate things they are utterly unaware.

Utterly. And so, one has to choose between philosophy and religion, as philosophy *is* a religion, *is* a way of seeing the world and a way of life based on that outlook, and any proposed solution that is rooted in that tradition will also indubitably be wrong, as it is founded on an approach that gives too wide a compass to reason, and does not provide any place at all for revealed truth, which should have pride of place in any outlook that is properly called religious.

> What indeed has Athens to do with Jerusalem? What concord is there between the Academy and the Church? . . . Our instructions come from "the porch of Solomon". . . . Away with all attempts to produce a mottled Christianity of Stoic, Platonic, and dialectic composition! We want no curious disputation after possessing Christ Jesus . . . ! — Tertullian, *Prescription Against Heretics* (VII)

Thus, *The History of Logos and the Logos of History*, which is the title of the book which E. Michael Jones is proposing, "a book which will allow us to get beyond the philosophical roadblock known as the English ideology and get back to a truly universal philosophy based on *Logos*", is bound to be yet another entry into the ping-pong ding-dong volley-fest otherwise known as Western Philosophy, and will not and cannot by definition be definitive, because once finality is claimed for something, once something is held as unfalsifiable, it exits the fold of critical thinking (based on pure reason alone). The point is, one cannot claim to be in possession of eternal truths (which I believe the Catholic Church certainly is, at least to some significant extent, its early history notwithstanding), and at the same time want to be part of a tradition whose presuppositions and methods are antithetical to that special and central faculty of cognition we know as revelation, and which is a square peg which does not fit into the round hole of philosophy. One cannot, in other words, set up shop as a "philosophical religion", and then limit what will and will not be acceptable as *kosher* or *halāl* philosophizing, as did John Paul II's *Fides et Ratio,* which "sets out a charter for philosophy as an aid to understanding the faith, based on the pre-suppositions made by St Thomas Aquinas for all philosophizing."[2]

Here are some of the volleys in the philosophical ping-pong that the Church engaged in *prior* to the hullabaloo of Kant's neumenon-phenomenon distinction:

> The conflict between Augustinian theology and Aristotelian philosophy was to lead to the greatest development in Western thought since Aristotle himself: St Thomas Aquinas's synthesis of these conflicting views in numerous works, culminating in the *Summa Theologiae*. But the initial response to the publication of Aristotle's works was to prohibit them, as happened in 1210 in Paris. The prohibition lapsed, but the incorporation of Aristotle into Christian thought remained controversial: St Bonaventure condemned Aristotelianism in his Eastertide lectures in 1273, and in 1277, three years after the death of Aquinas, Stephen Tempier, Bishop of Paris, condemned twenty propositions advanced by him. In 1289, the Franciscan Order prohibited the copying of the Summa without the incorporation of a text by William de la Mare condemning 117 of its propositions.[3]

And around Kant's time and onward:

> The dominant Catholic thinkers of the early nineteenth century – especially Antonio Rosmini (1797-1855) – were heavily indebted to Kantian ideas; Thomists were a disruptive minority. As late as 1865 a Jesuit Provincial described a statement of the Thomist position as 'a condemnation of the whole body of the Society and, what is worse, the Episcopate.'[4]

---

2 Joe Egerton, *Faith, Reason and the Modernists*, 2009.

3 Ibid.

4 Alasdair MacIntyre, *Three Rival Versions of Moral Enquiry* page 72; quoting Paolo Dezza Alle origini del neotomismo, Milano, 1960, page 60.

8. The "Curious Disputations" of Greek Philosophy

So *that* is how deep the rabbit hole runs: the crisis of the Catholic Church, which, in its denial, it thinks of as the problem of modernity (or used to, until it drank the Kool-Aid at its Second Council at the Vatican and embraced it), goes back way before the modern era, and back to the fact that the very scripture that it claims to represent, the message of Christ Jesus the son of Mary, is not even in the language that the Christ spoke! This is not a trifling matter. And certainly nothing to be proud of!! It goes back to the clash between Petrine and Pauline Christianity, and the "Jewish Christianity" of James and the issue of who was the rightful inheritor and vicar of Jesus' ministry (and whether or not Paul had any brief to universalize the Christ's teachings, or whether they were meant only for the tribe of Israel as a stepping stone between the Mosaic dispensation and that of the revelation of the Quran which is meant to have truly universal applicability). But that is a story for another day.

But then, in the chapter entitled the Family of Imrān, in a passage where He talks about "those who are bent on denying the truth" and who are allured by all of the pleasures of this world, Almighty God states that "All this may be enjoyed in the life of this world - but the most beauteous of all goals is with God." He then proceeds to provide us with the alternative:

> [3:15-18] Say: "Shall I tell you of better things than those [earthly joys]? For the God-conscious there are, with their Sustainer, gardens through which running waters flow, therein to abide, and spouses pure, and God's goodly acceptance." And God sees all that is in [the hearts of] His servants – those who say, "O our Sustainer! Behold, we believe [in Thee]; forgive us, then, our sins, and keep us safe from suffering through the fire"– ; those who are patient in adversity, and true to their word, and truly devout, and who spend [in God's way], and pray for forgiveness from their innermost hearts. God [Himself] proffers evidence – as do the angels and all who are endowed with knowledge – that there is no deity save Him, the Upholder of Equity; and that there is no deity save Him, the Almighty, the Truly Wise.

And Almighty God tells us that the only religion acceptable to him is Islam and that all of the quarrelling among those communities of faith that were vouchsafed revelation earlier, and all of the philosophizing and failure to reach consensus on a single first principle among their leaders was through envy of each other; and He ends with a severe note of caution:

> [3:19] Behold, the only [true] religion in the sight of God is Islam [i.e. man's self-surrender unto His *sharī'a* and Providential Lordship]; and those who were vouchsafed revelation aforetime took, out of mutual jealousy, to divergent views [on this point] only after knowledge [thereof] had come unto them. But as for him who denies the truth of God's messages – behold, God is swift in reckoning!

All of the above criticisms of Christianity have been at the level of its superstructure, leaving its scriptural basis alone. But unfortunately, the Bible is full of contradictions. And this is because it does not represent the original revelations, but rather, is a document which has been tampered with over and over again (in the case of the Old Testament, which is a late redaction of an indeterminate and hence unreliable oral tradition), and is a chronicling of events by mutually contradictory chroniclers of unknown origin and of dubious authenticity which certainly cannot pass the bar of being the equivalent of a revealed truth that is self-consistent and immaculate which can be relied on with certainty for the guidance of humanity. For example, Jesus is reported by Mark [12:29] to have taught that "The Lord our God is one [= singular, unitary, unique]"; and when he is said by Mark to have said this, he is doing nothing other than reaffirming that which was asserted earlier in Deuteronomy 6:4 "Hear, O Israel: The Lord our God, the Lord is one." Yet, because of other accretions in the overall text, the Christian creed asserts that Jesus was "God-incarnate", and they explain this by stating that he was "fully man" and "fully God" at one and the same time. But as we saw in the above proof, man is a finite, bounded, created entity, whereas God is infinite, unbounded, and uncreated, i.e. He is of a different nature altogether than man. And as another rational proof, as Arius has stated,

> "If, said he, the Father begat the Son, he that was begotten [must have] had a beginning of existence; hence it is clear that there was [a time] when the son was not."

So it is obvious that there is a massive logical contradiction in the

8. The "Curious Disputations" of Greek Philosophy

very heart of the Christian creed which cannot be resolved by any way other than to discard the doctrine of the incarnation *in toto* and come back to the original teachings in Mark 12:29 and Deuteronomy 6:4, whose originality is obviated by the fact that they are logical and do not violate our sense of reason. All our Christian brothers and cousins in faith need to bear in mind is that God, being infinite, is Eternally Self-Sufficient and Absolute (the All-Embracing Uncaused Cause of All Being Who stands in need of none and of Whom all are in need) (*as-Samad*), whereas being "fully human" means the absence of divinity; means being dependent, not Self-Sufficient and not Absolute. Of course, that having been said, there is nothing preventing Jesus from being an *immaculate epiphanic manifestation* of God, which is the correct position. Jesus, like all of the other Great Prophets, was a Perfect Man, and was chosen for this reason by God and sent to humanity as a perfect example of how He expects us to be, of what He expects us to aspire to. That is the Islamic position, which is perfectly logical. Given this, the Quran, which is the Final Testament which was sent down from on high in order to resolve all of the contradictions that crept into past revelations, then poses a question to those in the Family of Man who have not as yet attained to faith in it:

أَفَلَا يَتَدَبَّرُونَ الْقُرْآنَ وَلَوْ كَانَ مِنْ عِندِ غَيْرِ اللَّهِ

لَوَجَدُوا فِيهِ اخْتِلَافًا كَثِيرًا

> [4:82] Will they then not ponder the Quran? Had it issued from any source but God [Himself], they would surely have found in it many internal contradictions!

And as a final word on the subject before we move on, let us just say that one cannot claim to be in possession of eternal truths, and at the same time want to be part of a tradition whose creedal bases and presuppositions are antithetical to simple logic, and whose textual basis is so ridden with breaches in the integrity of its chain of custody as to be unsalvageable, i.e. as to have no integrity whatsoever from any rational vantage. The eras where Christianity can get away with that kind of "mystery religion" are over, as it is as clear as day even to the vast majority of those who consider themselves to be Christian, that this kind of thing is nothing more than an outdated form of mystagogery.

The European New Right - A Shia Response

And again, one cannot lay claim to be providing the most intricate, advanced and sophisticated sociological and geopolitical analysis of the current political situation of the world, and at the same time claim to believe in tenets which are patently false and bereft of any and all logic. The insights of Enlightenment thinkers such as Voltaire and Hume concerning religion itself were superficial and false, but the critique of such early advocates of the historical or scientific and critical study of the Bible such as Ferdinand Christian Baur and the Tubingen school of biblical criticism which subjected Christianity to a critical historical examination cannot be ignored or swept under the carpet. We are with the rationalism of the Enlightenment on this issue, just as we are with Martin Luther's correct advocacy of making the Bible available in the vernacular of the common folk (as it had always been in Christian Orthodoxy), and against the testosterone-driven elitism of exclusive clerical access to sacred scripture. And we are all for full disclosure on the part of the Vatican concerning its library, to which biblical scholars should be given full access, so that the true history of the early development of Christianity can finally come to light, not least concerning the Gospel of Barnabas. These critiques of Christianity are unassailable and are levelled at it at its most basic level, such that any thinker of conscience cannot ignore these criticisms in this day and age without being subject to the ignominious charge of irrationality. The scriptural basis of Islam, on the other hand, is immune to such criticisms;[5] subsequently, the cosmology and metaphysics that it reveals is able to overcome errors which Christianity and secular humanism have not been able to avoid. It is impossible for Western man to go back to the Christian scripture, which has been superseded and discredited by the positive aspects of rational Enlightenment thought. And it is equally impossible for Western man to change the bounds of the sacred law (*sharī'a*) of Islam. But what *is* possible is for all of the positive aspects of Western civilization to be applied to what the Islamic community knows of how to live life within the bounds of the sacred law, so that this understanding is deepened, and so that a more profound, humane and more ethical civilization emerges as a result of the infusion of the positive aspects of Western civilization. Let us now see how the Quranic worldview resolves some of these deep-seated errors.

---

5 See *The Immunity of the Quran to Distortion & Falsification.* Abdol-Rahīm al-Mūsawī et al, Lion of Najaf Publishers, 2017.

9. Alain de Benoist contra the Totalitarians

Unlike Alexander Dugin and Michael Jones, Alain de Benoist openly recognizes the errors of Christianity and sees that it is no longer a path that is open to a rational man. And because he has been put off by Christianity's muddying the clear waters of monotheism, he has not given Islam the careful examination that is its due. And I hasten to add that the fault is with the community of Moslems as much if not more than that of Christianity, because from the very outset, i.e. from within moments of the death of the Prophet (and even before that, during his dying days when they were in preparation) the Moslem executed a *coup d'état* that derailed Islam from the course intended for it by God and His Prophet, such that all of the wars of conquest that took place under the Omayyads and even under the so-called "Rightly Guided" caliphs (Abu Bakr, Omar and Othmān) were and remain illegitimate from the Shi'a point of view. Not a single one of the Imams, including not least Imam Ali, participated in any of them or sanctioned them, and viewed them and the "regimes" (to use a neologism) who instigated them as illegitimate.[1] But whatever the reason, Alain de Benoist has not given Islam the careful examination that is its due. But nevertheless, he is ahead of Alexander Dugin and Michael Jones and the *Sede Vacantists* in that he has climbed down the tree from a branch that is dead or dying and which is about to snap at any moment; but once he reached the main trunk, rather than climb back up, he continued his descent, following that rascal philosopher Friedrich Nietzsche, down to the lower branches of the superstitions of Greek philosophy and their other pantheons. Brother Dugin also continued his descent, following Martin Heidegger, but like Turkey, he is somewhat schizophrenic, as his heart is with Christianity and remains lodged in the crook of that branch, but his mind is down in the darkness of a "pre-ontological" chaos, away from the dreaded totalitarian and exclusivist tyranny of *logos*, while his hands are groping in the dark for a firm handhold called the Fourth Political Theory. Benoist, for his part, asserts from his vantage – which is an amalgam of the pantheism of pagan Europe and the polytheism of ancient Greece – that *logos* was itself originally

---

[1] For a detailed exposition of this issue, the gentle reader is referred to Chapter 7 of *Creedal Foundations of Walīyic Islam*, Lion of Najaf Publishers, 2017.

just another expression of *mythos* as "the image of the idea precedes and is frequently more pregnant than its discursive formulation". This type of "mythic" thinking is very alluring to the sophisticated rationalists who don't necessarily see the limitations of reason but *sense* it, yet have not seen or for whatever reason do not want to see or enter into the door of Divine Revelation. The mentality is nicely gathered in the oh-so-sophisticated Princeton/Bollingen Mythos Series in World Mythology, which is authored by the likes of Eliade, Corbin, Malinowski, Jung, the Perennialists, etc. whose sole claim to fame is that they have taken the detection and gathering and classification of bizarre patterns in the human psyche not so much to the level of an art as to that of a religion. But to Benoist's main point concerning the issue of logos, we have devoted a chapter of its own, to which we shall get to before too long.

Michael O'Meara correctly summarizes de Benoist's criticism of Christianity's ontology and cosmology: "The immediate real was thus taken as incomplete, given that the true sources [*sic*; the plural is in the original] of being lay elsewhere." The implication throughout all of the Benoistist literature is that the immediate is *not* incomplete, and that the source (or sources) of being lie in the immediate here and "now; a variation of pantheism." We would respond that this is simply not the case, and that the world is nothing but a miniscule portion of the enormous magnitude of what the true reality that lies beyond the veil of death actually is. Death is the momentous event in the life of the individual where he or she will wake up to the true reality of what being *actually* is, and enter into the intermediary world of the *barzakh*[2], as the newborn exits the womb and enters into the world. Thus, here is yet another major difference: for us, life is to be lived as if it is a Prelude, whereas for the materialists who have failed to see beyond the veil of death into a reality that is incomparably more real, life is to be lived as if it is the Final Act.

On one hand, the West has become so fragmented, so used to fragmentary existence and all of the false diversity that it engenders; and on the other hand, it has seen the horrors of and borne the brunt of what I guess I will have to call "false totality" ideologies such as the "totalitarian" regimes of fascism, national socialism, communism

---

[2] See the chapter on the Barzakh, below, for a full explication of this key concept.

9. Alain de Benoist contra the Totalitarians

and liberalism, that it has come to think of a system that offers a "true totality" of life solutions, i.e. a truly integral system whereby life can and should be transacted in a way that is in accord with man's primordial disposition (*fetra*) as "a system of thought that ideologically reduces the whole of social reality to a single truth, a single way of life, a single manifestation of good and evil" (Benoist). Benoist has been conditioned to think of this as a bad thing, or just does so because of his Nietzschean yearning for Dionysus and the pre-Christian pantheon of the Greeks. Well, the only way we can respond to that, as it is a matter of an aesthetic and spiritual predilection rather than something that can be resolved by rational means, is that this is a major point of difference between not just Islamic monotheism and Greek polytheism, but between Islamic monotheism and what is thought of as Christian monotheism. To us Shi'a, our Christian cousins' monotheism is incomplete and hence mingled with *sherk* (usually translated as idolatry or polytheism), as is, to a much lesser extent, the *towhīd* or monotheism of our Sunni brothers in faith. And this is because in the Shi'a creedal definition of *towhīd*, it is contrasted with *sherk*, where *sherk* is defined as assigning partners alongside or as co-equals to God; idolatry; polytheism; paying obeisance to anything other than God. Here is the key point that is germane to the issue of an integral (or "totalitarian") religious prescription and playbook compared to a fragmentary and polyvalent one: Islamic monotheism revolves around fidelity (*towhīd*) and infidelity (*sherk*) to the Exclusivity of God's Providential Lordship in the social order of His Creation, where providence is defined as God's intervention in the world, and as the exercise of care and guidance by God in managing human affairs; God's commands as to how one shall and shall not live one's life and how we are to form and manage the public sphere. This is a reference to the creedal tenet within Shi'a Islam known as the Unicity of Providential Lordship (*towhīd-e rububīa^t*), which is the belief in the sovereignty of God over man as all-encompassing Law-giver. The creedal tenet entails the taking on of the yoke of the dominion of the *sharī'a^t* or of God's sacred revealed law by whose principles and ordinances one transacts one's individual and social life. In any event, we say that this is an important issue but one that ultimately has to do with one's aesthetic and spiritual predilection because once the Islamic vision of what it means to be a monotheist is manifested and made available to the extent that it has as a result of the revelations received by the Prophet Mohammad, and by his paradigmatic example and that of the Imams, then it is a poor sensibility indeed who cannot see this brilliant Mohammadan sun whose spiritual gravity orders the whole solar system, but prefers instead to squint and try to rediscover the various dim stars or superstitions within the chaotic Greek pantheon.

10. From Unipolarity to Multipolarity

So, going back to the basic distinction between absolute and conditional reality, we can say that the Islamic worldview is completely infused with this distinction. The word *towhīd* which is usually translated as Islamic monotheism or simply as monotheism is the first creedal principle of Islam. One has to believe in this principle in order to be a Moslem. Now Islamic monotheism is very different from its Christian counterpart in that we believe that there is only one God, Who is the Creator, but we also believe that God has a will, and has created creation in such a way as to enable each person to make the choice of whether or not to submit his or her will to that of God's, which is made known in no uncertain terms and is comprehensive and integral in that it covers every aspect of how one is to lead one's life.

Towhīd, then, posits not only that there is only one deity, but that He has providential lordship over all of His creation, including that of man's affairs; and that all of the orders of creation, from mineral to vegetable to animal and to man, are seamlessly integrated into God's creation and innate will, which, in the case of man who has been given limited free will, is exercised through God's revealed sacred laws and His providential lordship. Man's fetric nature (his primordial or original disposition) is *towhīdic*; that is, it is in harmony with the ontic unicity or existential oneness of God; it is monotheistic: it is naturally inclined toward and accepts God's sovereignty over him and is innately inclined to serve only He who is his Maker. The most important tenet within the creedal principal of towhīd within Shi'a Islam is the creedal tenet known as the Unicity of Providential Lordship (*towhīd-e rububīaᵗ*), which is the belief in the sovereignty of God over man as all-encompassing Law-giver and entails the taking on of the Yoke of the Dominion of the sharīᵗaᵗ or God's sacred revealed law by whose ordinances and tenets one transacts one's individual and social life.

There is only *one* absolute being, and He has a certain nature and will and way and that will and way is infused in the fabric of His Creation. That will and way is singular, and because we are beings who are free but not independent, the nature of our choice is either that we can conform our will to that of our Maker and board the ship, as it were, which is sailing to our salvation in the world to come which is free from the constraints of time; or we can choose to do otherwise, in which case, we will have distanced ourselves from that which is real and everlasting and will perish like everything else that has been created by God but which is not invested in God's will and purpose.

When the Quran states that there is no deity other than God (or Allāh), it also makes clear that what is meant is that *there is nothing that is truly real other than Allāh*. Allāh is the only absolute reality, in other words. That is the meaning of the first part of the Moslem's profession of faith: *lā ilāha illā Allāh*: there is no deity [= true reality] other than Allāh. This is not to say that His creation is not real. Indeed, it is very real. Our intent in this definition is not to take away from that. But every moment of our reality is dependent on God's will; and as God is the only reality that is not dependent on anything, it is thus an absolute rather than a contingent reality. Everything in creation owes its being to Allāh. Every being, be it from the mineral, vegetable or animal kingdom, is a dependent being, and as such, is not real in a true sense, as its being is dependent on the will and whim of God, and is limited by time, being a created entity whose being is within time and encompassed by time, i.e. is limited by and bounded in time. It is only those beings who pass the test of time-bound life who will attain to an existence that is real, unconditional, and endless. And those who fail the test will pass away into obscurity and nothingness (after having paid for whatever sins they committed during the test which they failed).

Thus, the true and actual nature of the world is unipolar in the sense that there is only one God, and He has created creation in a certain way that is in conformance with His will; and at the level of the human domain, any human being who conforms his or her life transaction to that will, will therefore have lived a moral life, and anyone who does not do so will have lived a life that is less than moral. God created us with a faculty of understanding which is referred to as *'aql* in the Quran, which tells us that this faculty is not sufficient on its own and stands in need of guidance. This guidance, including the use of language, was provided by God to Adam and Eve, who then taught it to their offspring. (We go into some detail concerning this faculty in the chapter entitled *Logos and the Analogy of the Light of the Eye* which appears further down.) Thus, at the dawn of the history of humanity, mankind was united in what they believed in, and consequently, in how they were to transact their lives:

10. From Unipolarity to Multipolarity

[2:213] All mankind were once one single community; [then they began to differ -] whereupon God raised up the prophets as heralds of glad tidings and as warners, and through them bestowed revelation from on high, setting forth the truth, so that it might decide between people with regard to all on which they had come to hold divergent views. Yet none other than the selfsame people who had been granted this [revelation] began, out of mutual jealousy, to disagree about its meaning after all evidence of the truth had come unto them. But God guided the believers unto the truth about which, by His leave, they had disagreed: for God guides onto a straight way him that wills [to be guided].

So, just to recap: the Islamic view is that there is only one deity (whose proper name is Allāh), that it is only this deity and His will that are real in the sense that He and His will are independent, self-sufficient and absolute, and as such, are the only things that are ever-lasting.

[112:1] Say: "He is the One (*ahad*) God:

[112:2] "God the Eternally Self-Sufficient and Absolute (the All-Embracing Uncaused Cause of All Being Who stands in need of none and of Whom all are in need) (*as-Samad*).

[112:3] "He begets not, nor is He begotten;

[112:4] "and there is nothing that could be compared with Him."

And we explained that it is also a creedal belief of Islam that God's will and way are infused in His Creation, and that there is only one way to attain to an ontic status where we are free from the constraints of time and mortality, and that is to conform our will to that of God's, as He is the only Being Who is real, and as we are not ontically independent and real, in order to become so, we must hitch our wagons, as it were, to His powerful and almighty horses. Thus, from an Islamic standpoint, the reality of Creation is unipolar. There is only one God, one pole; and there is only one nature and one way: His. The animal, vegetable and mineral kingdoms conform to His will, as do the angels, but we have been given a limited amount of latitude in this temporary domain of existence, in this *donyā* or lower world. We are free to choose to live a life of righteousness and conform our lives to the way in which He has willed us to live (which will He has communicated

The European New Right - A Shia Response

to us through His prophets through the ages, the last of whom was the Chosen (*al-Mostafā*) Most Noble Prophet Mohammad (may peace and blessings be showered upon him and upon the Purified and Immaculate members of his House). The nature and fabric of Creation are such that if we decide to do so, our decisions will naturally result in a spiritual proximity to the one and only Source of Perpetuity, and if we chose to live a life that is contrary to His will and contrary to Truth and Justice, then we will have distanced ourselves from that source, and will, by definition, wither away after judgement day and after having paid for our sins, (unless God in His infinite Grace, intervenes or allow others to intercede on our behalf).

Because Islam envisions the order of creation as being integral, the social or political sphere is seamlessly integrated into the moral and even the metaphysical domains, such that every element in each domain is interconnected with each other. Thus, the original unity of creed and purpose which obtained at the time of Adam and Eve can and should rightly be described as the original state of unipolarity, because it was in conformance and harmony with the unchanging moral and metaphysical reality that is in God and which is infused in His creation and which constitute the warps and woofs of its very fabric.

This original and *actual* "unipolar moment" was shattered when Kane murdered Able, at the dawn of human history. What is important to realize when we talk about unipolarity and multipolarity is to recognize the actual nature of the order or orders we are talking about. The same applies to discussions about the "New" World Order as opposed to the Old World Order. What exactly are we talking about here? It's OK to talk about these matters on a political, sociological, military, or geostrategic level. But if we want to get to the heart of the matter, we need to talk about the nature of order itself, which is a philosophical and in our view a theological discussion. And it is OK, we suppose, to talk about order at these superficial levels, and at levels where secular science has fragmented and atomized science itself into various compartments which correspond to the various faculties within the universities of the modern world. But this approach can never yield satisfactory results, because the world itself is, by its nature, integral and interconnected; so that just as it is the case that if we are to attempt to transact our lives in a way that truly integrates our social affairs with our moral beliefs, we must integrate the tenets of our religion

10. From Unipolarity to Multipolarity

with the institutions of our state; in a similar way, if we are to attempt to understand the whole world, which is integral and undivided in its ultimate nature, we must necessarily integrate the knowledge and learning of the seminaries with that of the universities. Thus, what is required is a process of the resacralization of knowledge.

Be that as it may, the first creedal principal of Islam, *towhīd*, tells us that there is only one deity, and that this deity (whose proper name is Allāh[1]) created the world in accordance with a certain *order*. *That* order is the *Old* World Order, the Godly order; and it is this order which the "New" Word Order is juxtaposed against (and trying to change). This world order obtains in the mineral, vegetable and animal domains, which is why everything works beautifully like clockwork at the level of those domains (except when man interferes with it). But one of the features of the highest domain within creation *in potentia* i.e. that of mankind, is that mankind has been created with a limited amount of free will. God's purpose in doing so is to test us to see which of His creatures are deserving of everlasting happiness and which are not, and the means by which this test is carried out has to do with man's choosing to lead a moral life or his or her failure so to choose. But that discussion will take us far afield of where we want to go. The salient point to bear in mind with respect to the issue of multipolarity is that the order of creation is infused with and permeated with morality, which is an integral part of the fabric of creation. Thus the world order – the *old* world order – is an inherently *moral* order. And as has already been adumbrated, the moral order of the world – how man is to live out his life in this world – was communicated by God to Adam when He taught him "all the names".

> [2:31] And He imparted unto Adam the names of all things; then He brought them within the ken of the angels and said: "Declare unto Me the names of these [things], if what you say is true." [2:32] They replied: "Limitless art Thou in Thy glory! No

---

[1] Incidentally, all of the Christians in the heartland of the monotheistic religions, i.e. from Palestine and the Levant to Arabia, refer to their God as Allāh. It is only those who have strayed far afield who refer to Him by other names. A similar analogy can be seen in the way Christians pray. The Quran tells us that the Virgin Lady Mary and Zakarīya prayed in the way Moslems pray, and this is confirmed by the fact that if you visit the oldest Christian monasteries which are located in Syria, you will see the Christian monks bow down and prostrate themselves to Allāh when engaged in their devotional prayers.

knowledge have we save that which Thou hast imparted unto us. Verily, Thou alone art all-knowing, truly wise." [2:33] Said He: "O Adam, convey unto them the names of these [things]." And as soon as [Adam] had conveyed unto them their names, [God] said: "Did I not say unto you, 'Verily, I alone know the hidden reality of the heavens and the earth, and know all that you bring into the open and all that you would conceal'?" [2:34] And when We told the angels, "Prostrate yourselves before Adam!" - they all prostrated themselves, save Iblis, who refused and gloried in his arrogance: and thus he became one of those who deny the truth.

So, knowledge of all things was instilled into the heart of Adam (may God's peace be unto him), including the knowledge of how to live a moral life; and Adam then proceeded to impart this knowledge to Eve and their progeny. But man, having Fallen (into the *donyā* or the lower world, which is the Testing Ground and Tiling Field of the Hereafter or of the Higher World or the world which has a much higher level of ontic intensity), must choose to listen to his reason and revelation or, alternately, to listen to his lower urges and desires, and has been given the capacity to do the latter. And it is the Kanes of the world which choose not to follow their reason and divine guidance, and do harm to their own souls and to that of others by so doing. God, by His mercy and grace, has commissioned hundreds of prophets through the ages in order to remind mankind of who we are, where we came from, and where we are heading. But alas, none of them were given a proper hearing, and most of them were simply murdered.

The world is created in a way whereby a certain *order* obtains, and this order includes a moral dimension which obtains at the level of the human being on the social as well as on the individual level. But humans, being free agents, choose not to abide by that social order, choosing to rebel against it, like the jinn Iblīs, who was the first to rebel. Kane was the first human being to rebel against God's moral order by killing his brother Abel. And it was because of Kane's choice, and the choice of those who followed in his footsteps that the family of man was fragmented into different "poles", each competing with the other for advantage and supremacy rather than living in God's harmony as one integral family.

11. From Multipolarity Back to Unipolarity

In the New Horizon conference, Brother Alexander talked in terms of these emergent poles and civilizations as having their own independent ontic realities, so that what we are witnessing, he claimed, was the emergence of multiple poles which were not only politically and economically independent, but which had their own *ontic* realities. But this is not the case. There is only *one* reality, and there can only *be* one reality: that which was created by God when He created creation. And that is the reason why the "New" World Order is doomed to fail, ultimately. But let us move, for the sake of the argument, from the actual, metaphysical level, to the theoretical one and try to envision more than one ontic reality. When we do this, we see immediately that multiple ontic realities can never yield order but only chaos, which is a state that is best described as the absence of order and which does not have any value in terms of order (which is what we are talking about) inasmuch as and insofar as *chaos* obtains. What I said to Brother Alexander in response to his presentation on multipolarity is that the problem is that the communications protocols and interfaces of different civilizations or "poles" are different from each other *by definition*. In other words, it is the very differences and incompatibilities of different civilizations and "humanities" (his word) which define their boundaries. Thus, (continuing our thought experiment), we see that without these proper and necessary communications protocols and interfaces, *order* will never obtain. In other words, the phrase "multipolar *order*" is a contradiction in terms. This is the meaning of the following two Quranic *āyas*:

لَوْ كَانَ فِيهِمَا آلِهَةٌ إِلَّا اللَّهُ لَفَسَدَتَا

فَسُبْحَانَ اللَّهِ رَبِّ الْعَرْشِ عَمَّا يَصِفُونَ

[21:22] Had there been in heaven or on earth any deities other than God, both [those realms] would certainly have fallen into disorder and ruin! But limitless in His glory is God, enthroned in His awesome almightiness [far] above anything that men may devise by way of definition!

The European New Right - A Shia Response

مَا اتَّخَذَ اللَّـهُ مِن وَلَدٍ وَمَا كَانَ مَعَهُ مِنْ إِلَـٰهٍ ۚ إِذًا لَّذَهَبَ كُلُّ إِلَـٰهٍ بِمَا خَلَقَ وَلَعَلَا بَعْضُهُمْ عَلَىٰ بَعْضٍ ۚ سُبْحَانَ اللَّـهِ عَمَّا يَصِفُونَ

> [23:91] Never did God take unto Himself any offspring, nor has there ever been any deity side by side with Him: [for, had there been any,] lo! each deity would surely have stood apart [from the others] in whatever it had created, and they would surely have [tried to] overcome one another [thereby bringing about a state of utter chaos]! Limitless in His glory is God, [far] above anything that men may devise by way of definition.

And this, dear Professor, is the meaning of monotheism. And so I told Brother Alexander that what we are witnessing is precisely the *opposite* of what he posited: the world is not moving from a unipolar moment to a multipolar one; rather, the world has been multipolar from the time of Kane and Able, in a state of multipolar disorder, and has remained so despite the commissioning of hundreds of prophets; and is, rather, moving from the chaos of the multipolar world to the order and integrality of unipolarity or the true monotheism intended by God for His creatures. But as we have more than amply demonstrated, we are not capable of bringing a unipolar state back on our own; without the aid, that is, of the Universal Savior. And that is why the texture and feel of the era which we have entered into with the collapse of the Grand Narrative is eschatonic. But before we pursue that line of thought to its logical conclusion, let us say a word or two about the failure itself, the nature of the failure.

It is natural for Brother Alexander and the Eurasianists and Grecists to advocate multipolarity and "particularism", because they are reacting against the worldwide extension and the universalization of the liberals and their supposed egalitarianism, which is nothing other than a secularized version of the *logos* of the defunct and discredited Catholic Church (which has added insult to injury and further disgraced itself with the broadside it self-inflicted in its Second Vatican Council where it capitulated to the attacks of Kant and Hume and agreed to their terms of peace); and the placing of an Age of Reason secular-humanist head on the rationalist-universalist body of scholasticism and the Thomist synthesis of the *Summa*. We agree that it is absurd to want to impose this *particular* uniform model of humanity on the

11. From Multipolarity Back to Unipolarity

entire planet. Again, the problem is not with the concept of a universal model *per se*. The nature of the world *is* uniform, as we explained above. And not only *is* it uniform, it cannot be anything *but* unitary and uniform, for else, there will be nothing but chaos. But in no way can this uniform model be that of the liberal universalists. But equally, the alternative model or models that are to be pursued cannot and should not be "particularist" and based on a relativist ontology, as this is at variance with the reality of the world. What each of us needs to do is to pursue our own universalist tradition while not imposing it by force or economic coercion on others as is the wont of the liberal New World Order crowd, knowing that what we are engaged in is a project that cannot succeed; and pray and trust in the Second Coming of the Christ Jesus, (and of the Imam al-Mahdi, in the case of those living within the Islamic tradition), upon whose advents the unitary, integral universal order that was intended for man but which man alone cannot bring about will be established, God willing.

Adopting this posture of active awaiting (*entezār*) will allow us to maintain a metaphysics which is in accord with the reality of the world of creation and an epistemology that is solidly grounded on bedrock, while also enabling us to respect and honor and legitimate the vast range of cultural diversity that obtains within the various civilizations that have arisen since the time Kane slew Abel. Thus, in a very important sense, we in the Shi'a citadel (which is, after all, "Ground Zero" in the fight against liberal universalism) give you, our fellow comrades in arms the glad tidings that it is not necessary to abandon the two most basic elements and components of your millennial traditions in the fight to uphold your millennial traditions, i.e. the dualist ontology of God and His Creation, and the foundationalist and universalist epistemology that is grounded in His revelation and reason. The only thing that needs to be jettisoned is the Crusading spirit of wanting to impose this worldview on others *by coercion and force*. (Even the impetus of wanting to impose it is not problematic and we would say is even necessary; but this must be done by way of rational debate and reasoned argument in a civilized and peaceable fashion.)

Unlike the view that sees the world's multifarious expressions achieving coherence through the imposition of a specific cultural stylization, universalism assumes that the particular is an imperfect variant of the general, that behind the world's innumerable contingencies and differences there lies an ahistorical, transcultural essence linking them all, and that the universal is necessarily superior to the particular.

The truth is that the assumptions of the schoolmen and of Islam are correct: there *is* an ahistorical, transcultural essence which connects all of the innumerable cultural variations in human history. It is that trans-temporal eschaton whose *telos* is what gives meaning to human history. But it is God's sublime humility and praiseworthy modesty (*hayā*) that prevents Him from putting this "in our faces"; and so He lets us find this out gradually, through a process of self-disclosure which began with the Prophet Adam and ended with the Seal of the Prophets, the Prophet Mohammad; and after that, for those who still have not paid heed to that message, by a process of allowing humanity to do what it believes to be right (contra divine guidance), and for it to come up against frustration after frustration, as anything that we do that is at variance with that which is true and real and just (*al-haqq*) is null and void (*al-bātel*), and as such, is bound to come to naught and to perish.

Thus, with the liberal universalists, we also claim that any particularistic identity which separates the individual from the brotherhood of humanity and the part from the whole are transitory and "bound to perish",[1] bound to give way to "that which pertains to all," just as we are bound to evolve into a single brotherhood which reflects our common humanity. But the difference is that we see this happening only with the aid of divine intervention and after the advent of the Universal Savior, and thus we characterize the New World Order project of the liberals and neocons as a grotesque latter day form of what Eric Voeglin used to refer to as "the imminantization of the Eschaton"; that is, imminantizing that which is yet transcendent as its time has not yet come. Playing God with the world, in other words; or, in a single word: humanism.

And so, we agree with Brother Alexander Dugin in our refusal to accept the chimera of liberal universalism, but must disagree with him when they maintain that there is no essence inherent in the order of things, no sacred geometry that orders the world prior to the Advent in

---

1   Per [17:81] And say: "*al-haqq* has now come [to light], and *al-bātel* has [consequently] withered away: for, behold, [by its very nature] *al-bātel* is bound to perish!"

11. From Multipolarity Back to Unipolarity

a latent form despite the deeds of men, and which will frame the social affairs of humanity in accordance with God's will, so that mankind as a whole can and will live in peace as one. And we must disagree with Brother Alain de Benoist who, following the postmodernists, believes that such essences "derive from particularistic postulates that confuse a highly abstract generalization with an objective reality."[2] This is *not* a Prison Planet, and the world is *not* a crypt whose turnkey is some demiurge who gets his kicks out of human suffering. This is just a temporary "multipolar moment", if you will, the hardest test in human history, which is bound, inevitably, to give way to an era of universal peace and harmony.

Again: the world is not moving from a unipolar moment to a multipolar one; rather, the world has been multipolar from the time of Kane and Able, and is, rather, moving from the chaos of the multipolar world to the order and integrality of unipolarity or the true monotheism intended by God for His creatures. But as we are not capable of bringing a unipolar state back on our own, without the aid, that is, of the Universal Savior, this movement is taking place in a special way, in an eschatological way. Communism and Fascism and National Socialism failed, and the Liberal order is no better if not worse. Therefore, the various peoples and nations of the world want to tear away from it and establish their own "piece of Heaven", as it were; away from the tendrils and tentacles of the Leviathan and monster that Liberal Democracy has transmogrified into: a monster who wants to enslave all and to have all of humanity to work as slaves to satisfy the carnal pleasures of the sick individuals and families that are pulling the strings from behind the veil of the chimera which they project. But because the world and the order with which it was created are unitary, these individual efforts at escaping the Hegemon can never amount to anything, because they are all (and I include the Islamic Republic of Iran in this generalization, even though the IRI is a special category and an exception in certain ways) – because they are all trying to establish an order that is not in conformity with the created order of the world, and as such, they are all doomed to fail. And this is because the deeper the ontic density of each pole (if we grant for the sake of the argument that each pole can indeed have its own ontic independence),

---

2   Alain de Benoist, "Fondements nominalistes d'une attitude devant la vie," *Nouvelle École* 33 (Summer 1979).

then the more discombobulated will be the communications interfaces and protocols between each pole/ civilization/ "humanity". And each pole will naturally want to dominate the others as they grow stronger – which is a recipe for chaos not order. The Quran tells us that had there been more than one God,

> [23:91] lo! each deity would surely have stood apart [from the others] in whatever it had created, and they would surely have [tried to] overcome one another [thereby bringing about a state of utter chaos]!

Kane was the first secular humanist, and each pseudo-pole that has arisen since his time as a result of his rebellion and the rebellion of all mankind against God's order and against God's guidance, has "[tried to] overcome one another", which is why the history of mankind is a sordid history of the barbaric wars of peoples and nations and civilizations against one another. And again, this "multipolarity" is not an emergent world order, but a recipe for continued chaos.

Thus, we believe that what we are witnessing today, and what Ayatollah Khāmeneī has referred to repeatedly as the *pīch-e tārīkhī* (literally, "historical turn [of events]" or, *a momentous turn [in the history of mankind]*) *is an interregnum that is imbued with a deeply eschatological character*. And this is because the more we progress through this "momentous turn", the more each "pole" (or pseudo-pole, properly speaking) will fail in its efforts to free itself of the evil and anti-logosic Leviathan which is the so-called "New" World Order. Our *hadīth* reports tell us that we (the Axis of Resistance centered around the Islamic Republic of Iran, with the brotherly help of the Rus' People or the Third Rome, and with the help of the people of the Yemen) will fail in the war of the End Times which is centered on Syria. And the greater the magnitude and frequency our failures become, the more the impossibility of the situation will be obviated; and the greater the frequency of this crushing frustration and failure of those who are fighting alongside the righteous forces in the world in the Battle of the End Times, the more this failure will resonate in the heart of humanity as a whole, and the more we will awaken to the awareness that there is no solution to the problem. And this will in turn gradually develop into the consciousness that there is no *human* solution to the problem. In other words, *the incremental revelation of*

11. From Multipolarity Back to Unipolarity

the impossibility of the situation we are in functions to bring about the original religious consciousness in man that is the awareness of his limitations, dependence and mortality; the *function of* what Ayatollah Khāmeneī has called the Historical Moment and what I will call *the Vortex of Impossibility is to catalyze the consciousness in man of his dependence on a higher power and to move away from the self-satisfied and false sense of security of secular humanism toward the ineluctable need for a Universal Savior.* In other words, there is only one order and there can only be one order, and that order is the realization of God's will on Earth as it is in Heaven.

We in the East and the West, all of us who have faith in the one and only God, are the spiritual heirs of the children of Israel, who bore witness to the unicity of God, and covenanted to worship only Him:

> [2:133] Nay, but you [yourselves, O children of Israel,] bear witness that when death was approaching Jacob, he said unto his sons: "Whom will you worship after I am gone?" They answered: "We will worship thy God, the God of thy forefathers Abraham and Ishmael and Isaac, the One God; and unto Him we surrender ourselves."

And so, willingly or unwillingly, in these "postmodern" end times, the Vortex of Impossibility will act to bring about a consciousness in man which existed in premodern eras, of man's dependence on Providence. Thus, all of our failures to bring about a peace that is universal and lasting, to bring about an order where men can live as brothers and sisters with all their diversities as a Brotherhood of Man – all these failures are but harbingers of the Second Coming of the Christ and of the Imam al-Mahdī. The impossibility, in other words, acts as yet another Portal of Grace.

12. *Dasein* and the *Barzakh*

Heidegger rightly situates the human being in a time-bound context, positing his or her existence as "Dasein" ("being-t/here") i.e. as "situated human existence". And Brother Alexander correctly surmises that "in order to understand where this 'there' is located, we should point it out and make a basic, foundational gesture". Heidegger claims, in *Hegel's Phenomenology of Spirit* (Section 13b), for example, that "the original essence of being is time." That is good and well, as far as it goes. The difference that arises between his cosmologies and anthropologies and those of the Quran's relate to the next question which has to do with the nature of *where exactly we are situated*. In other words, yes, we are located in time; but where, pray, is time *itself* located?! For if we believe with the materialists that all there is, is time; then Heidegger's claim that "the original essence of being is time" would be correct. This is the type of thinking that those who have not been able to transcend the veil of the material world invariably resort to. But our "foundational gesture" is to locate ourselves and time itself *in the womb of the barzakh* (an Islamic keyword which we shall explain shortly). If one is able to step back with the aid of revelation and see the time-bound world for what it is: a miniscule speck in the vast unending canopy of being that is not finite like the world that is bounded by time but unending, and whose ontic amplitude and intensity is incomparably higher than the statistical density which we are used to experiencing in this, the Lower World (*donyā*), then one would indubitably conclude that "the original essence of being is [not] time [but *beyond* time]".

The very first verses of the Quran (after its *fāteha* or opening prayer) reads as follow:

> [2:1] Alif. Lam. Mim. [2:2] This Divine Writ – let there be no doubt about it – is [meant to be] a guidance for all those who are in awe of God. [2:3] *Who believe in [the existence of] the [domain of existence] which is beyond the reach of [ordinary] human perception* (al-ghayb); who are constant in prayer; and spend on others out of what We provide for them as sustenance.

The European New Right - A Shia Response

We see here in the very first sentence of the Quran (after its "Opening" Sūra, the *Fāteha*) that the Quran divides reality into two realms: one that is available to sense perception, and one that is beyond the ken of ordinary human perception – that domain which the Quran refers to as *al-ghayb*. This second domain includes the world of the hereafter, which consists of the unimaginably vast and endless domains of heaven and hell, as well as the intermediary realm known as the *barzakh*. This word is usually translated, in my view mistakenly, as "isthmus" or "the isthmus". While it is true that *barzakh* literally means isthmus (a narrow neck of land, bordered on both sides by water, connecting two larger bodies of land), and that it is even true that this analogy holds for one of the definitions of the *barzakh* in so far as it is an intermediate stage between this world and the hereafter, it is misleading to translate it as such, because the other more important definition, which is understood in the Arabic and other Islamic languages, is ignored; namely, that the *barzakh* is a class of reality that actually *encompasses* the reality of the *donyā* (i.e. of this, the lower world), and that some of the attributes of this world are attributes which it shares with that of the *barzakh*, which is a higher level and order of reality. These include any phenomena which do not have "extension" or dimension and cannot be measured or sensed by the senses, such as thought, imagination, dreams, intuition, visions and hallucinations. Henry Corbin used to refer to the *barzakh* as the "Imaginal World". But perhaps a better way to think of it is to think of it as the Shi'a magisters do, namely, that this world is the *womb* of the *barzakh*: in other words, we are in the *barzakh* while we are still "in the womb" (our world), but we enter it proper upon our death, upon which event its veil is lifted, as the veil of the world is gradually lifted from an infant once he or she exits his or her mother's womb. The Noble Prophet is authoritatively reported to have said about the relationship of this world to the *barzakh*: "This world is but a dream from which we awake upon our deaths."

Thus, what we would say is that it is absolutely correct and essential to place man's existence in his spacio-temporal context and not to define him in terms that abstract him from such an essential part of his or her being. But it is also essential to place that spacio-temporal context within the larger *barzakhic* context, and to further place that *barzakhic* context in the much larger context of the hereafter which is endless. The Quran responds that the time-bound world of being is

12. Dasein and the Barzakh

nothing but "play and amusement" compared to the vast reality that lies beyond the Veil of Death in the domain that is "beyond the ken of ordinary human perception" which the Quran refers to as *al-ghayb*, or that domain which is hidden from ordinary human perception:

> [57:20] Know, [O people,] that the life of this world is but a play and a passing delight, and a beautiful show, and [the cause of] your boastful vying with one another, and [of your] greed for more and more riches and children. Its parable is that of [life-giving] rain: the herbage which it causes to grow delights the tillers of the soil; but then it withers, and thou canst see it turn yellow; and in the end it crumbles into dust. But [the abiding truth of man's condition will become fully apparent] in the life to come: [either] suffering severe, or God's forgiveness and His goodly acceptance: for the life of this world is nothing but an enjoyment of self-delusion.

We are unbounded spiritual beings on a temporary sojourn in a time-bound material world. We are pilgrims in the sense that this earth-bound journey is the means which God has provided for us to choose to listen to Guidance from Above and to perfect ourselves thereby, or to reject Divine Guidance and to spend our time in "boastful vying with one another" in order to accumulate in our unbounded greed "more and more riches and children".

Tanzīh, Tashbīh, Ta'tīl

So let us zoom back out and see how this understanding of being which is informed by the higher orders of reality (be they the *barzakh* or the infinitely vaster domains of Heaven and Hell) pans out with respect to the issue of truth. O'Meara tells us that,

> "Unlike Cartesian reason, with its unfiltered perception of objective reality, Heidegger sees all thought as self-referential, informed by historical antecedents that are inescapable because they inhere to the only world Dasein knows. This leads him to deny rationalism's natural, timeless, ahistorical truths. *Like being, truth is necessarily historical* [my emphasis]. Heidegger consequently rejects modernity's Cartesian metaphysics, which posits *the existence of a rational order outside history* [again,

the emphasis is mine]. By reconnecting subject and object in their given temporality, he seeks to deconstruct modernity's allegedly objective cognitive order".

Heidegger believes that "like being, truth is necessarily historical" and therefore denies "the existence of a rational order outside history". We say that neither being nor truth are historical in their essence, as all things that are truly real obtain and exist only in God, Who, indeed, is none other than "the existence of a rational order outside history". In so far as He is utterly transcendent above all that we can ascribe to Him (*sobhānahū wa ta'ālā*, i.e. fully *tanzīh* on the spectrum of *tanzīh* and *tashbīh*), He is unknowable and therefore "the existence of a rational order outside history" is unknowable. In this event, all thought would correctly be characterized as self-referential and as being "informed by historical antecedents that are inescapable because they inhere to the only world Dasein knows". Thus, in this event, reality would be deprived of any purchase to be objective, and all human discourse would necessarily degenerate into self-referential babble or nonsense. But this is what the Moslem philosophers would characterize as agnosticism (*tanzīh*) or stretching the umbilicus of meaningful abstraction beyond the limit of sensibility and comprehension (*ta'tīl*). And they reject this position by virtue of the fact that while on one hand God, in His essence, is indeed sublimely and utterly transcendent above all that we can ascribe to Him, but on the other hand, there are aspects of His essence which have similitude with the world of His creation and are imminent in it. And this we know through His self-disclosure known as the Quran, which He has made "easy to comprehend" [54:17].

The fact that Heidegger as well as the whole post-modern movement have rebelled against the "exclusivity" of logos and against the Cartesian and modernist conception of objectivity is understandable. Concerning the presence of God or, in our context, of an objective reality *within* time and history, Islamic theology posits a spectrum on one side of which is *tanzīh*, where God is posited to be completely and utterly transcendent above all that we can ascribe to Him. Thus, at this end of the spectrum, God cannot be known (or, objective reality cannot and does not obtain). Hence, the rendering of agnosticism for *tanzīh*, which is pretty common.

12. Dasein and the Barzakh

Corbin has rendered this ontological posture as one of "transcendence and sublimity" and as "the divestment of the pure Essence". He explains: "The principle and source of being always transcends being, and can be discerned only from afar, per *viam negativam* (*tanzīh*)", that is to say through apophatic theology. William Chittick describes it as "transcendence or incomparability" with all created reality, and contrasts it with "immanence or resemblance (*tashbīh*)". He explains that "In one respect, *tanzīh* denotes the utter lack of commonality between [the Absolute Being] *wujūd* and non-existence or the fact that the Essence is inaccessible to the creatures. In another respect, *tanzīh* refers to a set of divine attributes that stress the difference between God and creation, while *tashbīh* designates another set that suggests a certain similarity". Chittick concludes that *tashbīh* – God's presence in the cosmos – overrules the effects of *tanzīh*, His absence from it."

Elsewhere, Corbin correctly describes the two ends of the spectrum as consisting of the "twofold dangers" of *tashbīh* (anthropomorphism) and *ta'tīl* (agnosticism or abstractionism). *Ta'tīl* is a description of the *tanzīh* end of the spectrum. Henry Corbin refers to the Mu'tazilites, who were a rationalist school in the early centuries of Islam, and tells us that their attitude is known in the history of dogma by the name of *ta'tīl*, "that is to say, it consists in depriving God of all operative action and ends finally in agnosticism." Or ends, in the case of Heidegger as well as the whole post-modern movement, in a subjectivist epistemology, which therefore denies any objectivity to reality, and consequently maintains a pluralist ontology.

Corbin makes an interesting observation that the meaning of the root word from which *ta'tīl* is derived was applied in ancient Arabic usage to the well without water and to the childless woman. In other words, like homosexuality, it is a sterile ontic posture or station. And so Corbin rightly sees the danger of falling into the traps which lie on either side of this metaphysical (ontological as well as epistemological) spectrum, and tells us that "it will be necessary to walk the narrow ridge between agnosticism and anthropomorphism (*ta'tīl* and *tashbīh*), between negation and the negation of negation". In a passage that is a gem of philosophical jargon and mystagogery, Corbin characterizes *tashbīh* as "the assimilation of that which is Manifested to its Manifestation", which is incomprehensible nonsense, and concludes by taking his nonsense to an even higher level:

Hence we have the dialectic of double negativity: the Principle is non-being and not non-being, not in time and not not in time, and so on. Each negation is true only on condition of being itself denied. The truth lies in the simultaneity of this double negation, whose complement is the dual action of the *tanzīh* (the subduction of the Names and operations from the supreme divinity in order to transfer them to the *hūdūd*, the celestial and terrestrial stages of his Manifestation), and the *tajrīd* (the isolation and re-projection of the divinity beyond his Manifestations).[1]

Daniele Perra tells us that "the great Iranist Henry Corbin recognized that there was continuity and not a break in the intellectual path [of Islamic theosophy] that led him to abandon the field of Western philosophy (and especially Heideggerian studies) to embrace that of Islamic theosophy." But unfortunately, Henry Corbin, this prodigious theosophical talent, didn't go far enough, and remained stuck in philosophy, albeit of an Iranian flavor, thanks mainly to his mentor, Allāme Seyyed Mohammad Hosayn Tabātabāī's penchant for philosophical speculation and speculative theology.

Symbol, Incarnation, Theophany

But getting back to this theological spectrum of *tashbīh* and *tanzīh*, it has been said with some justification that the Hindus err on the side of transcendence (*tanzīh*), maintaining that everything is only and merely symbolic of God, as He (or It) is not present in the world. The Christians err in the other direction (*tashbīh*), maintaining not only that God *can* be present in the world, but that He indeed did incarnate Himself. As stated earlier in our chapter on the critique of Christianity, this is an absurdist position, as it violates two of the three fundamental laws of logic: (1) the law of contradiction, (2) the law of excluded middle (or third), and (3) the principle of identity. In other words, one cannot be finite and infinite at one and the same time. This is a violation of the law of contradiction and the principle of identity, and is thus not a "mystery" or a "paradox" or anything along those lines, but a simple contradiction. The correct position, which is that of the

---

[1] All of the quotes of Henry Corbin's in this passage are taken from his *History of Islamic Philosophy*, Routledge; 1st edition (August 14, 2014).

12. Dasein and the Barzakh

Shi'a, based on the *hadīth* report corpus that goes back to the words and deeds of the Prophet and the Imams (on all of whom be God's peace and blessings), is that the reality concerning God's immanence or transcendence in the world is that He is neither fully imminent nor fully transcendent, but is transcendent (*tanzīh*) to the limit of (i.e. just short of) incomprehensibility (*ta'tīl*). What this translates to in laymen terms is that God, being infinite in His nature, cannot incarnate Himself in a finite form, because that would not be who He is. And He cannot incarnate Himself in His infinite form, because we, as finite beings, do not and would not have the *ontic capacity* to "contain" Him in such an infinite and hence uncontainable form. But neither is He fully absent, so that we can only conceive of Him as the confused mass of gods and symbolic forms that the Hindus conceive of God. Being All-Wise and loving and compassionate towards His creatures, He selects the most perfect specimens from among our species (who are Adam, and Eve, and the sons and daughters of Adam and Eve); these are perfect and immaculate examples of humanity, who are sinless and inerrant, and are neither incarnations of God nor mere symbolic representations, but *theophanic manifestations* of God which represent the utmost limit of our ontic capacity to comprehend Him.

Thus, absolute, objective truth obtains to the extent to which God is present in the world, or the extent to which He has communicated *al-haqq* (His truth and reality and justice) to His creatures, through his Quranic self-disclosure, and through His prophets and Imams through the ages, who are perfect theophanies of His essence and attributes, and are thus able to be vested in the station of God's vice-regency on Earth – a station that only they are vested in by virtue of their immaculacy (sinlessness and inerrancy) and by virtue of their being God's theophanic hierophants and *hojjats* [2] on earth.

Will to Power or Will to Faith

And to conclude, if we want to come back full circle to where we stated that contrary to Heidegger who believes that "like being, truth is necessarily historical" and who therefore denies "the existence of a rational order outside history"; we say that neither being nor truth

---

2 For a full treatment of this important key word of Shi'a Islam, see *Creedal Foundations of Walīyic Islam*, Chapter 5 *passim*, but especially Sections 5.2 and 5.4

The European New Right - A Shia Response

are historical in their essence, as all things that are truly real obtain and exist only in God, Who, is not only "the existence of a rational order outside history", but has infused this rational order *throughout* history by means of His prophets, the last and most perfect of whom was the Prophet Mohammad, and by means of the Twelve Immaculate Imams who were charged with explicating this rational order to those who would listen, and to implement God's order on Earth as it is in Heaven, in the event that there are sufficient souls who would pay heed to God's Final Message to humanity which he revealed through the Arch-Angel Gabriel to the Prophet Mohammad, onto whom be God's everlasting peace, and to join in the prophetic and imāmic struggle for the earthly implementation of God's will.

And so when Brother Alexander states that "the Fourth Political Theory is, at the same time, a fundamental ontological theory which contains the awareness of the truth of Being at its core", he has to decide whether "the awareness of the truth of Being at its core" is one where, as with Heidegger and the materialists, "the original essence of being is time", or whether the awareness of the truth and essence of Being at the core of his Fourth Political Theory is *not* time, but *beyond* time; whether the awareness of the truth and essence of Being is material and time-bound, or that infinite and sublimely transcendent entity Who created time and Who created timelessness; Who created being and non-being; and whether being is ultimately subjective or whether *being is umbilically dependent on the absolute objectivity which resides only in God*.

As Nietzsche put it, without the "Beyond" i.e. an ontology that accounts for the reality which is God, one cannot have meaning in any real sense, i.e. an objective meaning that is accessible to all of humanity, by which we can all be expected to live and by whose criteria we can therefore be judged. An ontology that fails to produce such *an objective basis for communal judgment* is ultimately nihilistic as it denies the possibility of the Day of Judgement, denies the possibility of Resurrection, of Heaven and Hell, and of everlasting life in the Hereafter. In such an ontological position, one can only have subjective and inter-subjective meaning (which is not objective), so it is a question of a will to power or a will to faith; or a will to materialist, hedonist, narcissist nihilism or a will to brotherly communal existence in this world and eternal felicity in the Hereafter.

13. Logos and the Light of the Eye

The word *logos* is like the word democracy; it has been used by so many different people in so many different ways that it has been turned into an empty vessel into which each person pours his or her own meaning; as such, it has become meaningless in itself. And so it is necessary to define that which we believe the word represents. Brother Heidegger says that whereas *phainomenon* means "that which shows itself, the self-showing, the manifest," *logos* signifies a discourse, the function of which is to *apophainesthai*, to "let see" or "make manifest" what the discourse it about.[1] Brother Dugin adds that "the agrarian metaphor of *logos* [is] a concept formed from the verb *legein* — that is, 'to harvest', and later receiving the sense of 'to think', 'to read', 'to speak'". We believe there are two major facets to the word *logos*. The first is the order of creation and the logic that is embedded within it and on the basis of which creation is created; and the second is the faculty of intellection which has the wherewithal to discern this innate logic and order. Now this second facet, the faculty of intellection has two distinct parts, which can in turn be thought of as the hardware and firmware of a system that enables meaning and understanding to obtain. Alternatively, the system can be thought of in terms of the metaphor of an eye (the hardware), and light (the firmware), without which light the eye cannot see.

From the Islamic perspective, mankind was made, like the rest of the orders within creation, in such a way as to be in harmony with the order that is innate to God's creation. But in addition to the other faculties which have been given to the lower orders of creation in the animal kingdom such as the faculty of sense, sight, hearing, etc., man has been given the faculty of intellection, which, as we just said, is bicameral. The first part corresponds to the Quranic term *'aql*, which can be thought of as the "hardware" of the faculty or of the "eye"; the second part is the instilling by God of the "firmware" into the faculty to enable it to run applications properly, or of the shining of the "light" onto the "eye" of the intellect so that the "eye" can see. In other words, we have a mental faculty of intellection (the "eye"), which is capable

---

1   *Being and Time*, page 32.

of reasoning (with the mind, its superficial level), and of receiving direct truth either through divine inspiration individually or through revelation generally (with the heart, its deeper core); but this faculty (or faculties, if you prefer) which we have likened to an eye, cannot function without there being any light for it to process. If we liken the faculty to a car, we would then say that the car cannot run without gas or petrol. Now this act of the instilling by God of the "firmware" into the faculty to enable it to run applications properly, or of the shining of the "light" onto the "eye" of the intellect *is an act of revelation*, which the Quran refers to as God's teaching Adam "all the names":

> [2:31] And He imparted unto Adam the names of all things; then He brought them within the ken of the angels and said: "Declare unto Me the names of these [things], if what you say is true." [2:32] They replied: "Limitless art Thou in Thy glory! No knowledge have we save that which Thou hast imparted unto us. Verily, Thou alone art all-knowing, truly wise." [2:33] Said He: "O Adam, convey unto them the names of these [things]." And as soon as [Adam] had conveyed unto them their names, [God] said: "Did I not say unto you, `Verily, I alone know the hidden reality of the heavens and the earth, and know all that you bring into the open and all that you would conceal'?"

It is not something that man learns or acquires through a gradual and constant process of trial and error. In other words, from the Islamic perspective, the dichotomy that exists in Western philosophical discourse that differentiates between reason and revelation is a false one: it is *all* revelation. It is just that the "firmware" or "light" that comprises the second half of the faculty of intellection (*'aql*) is a special kind of revelation that can be thought of in terms of its being an *initial* revelation; and further revelations which were revealed by God through His prophets can be thought of in terms of their being "firmware updates" which are necessitated due to viruses being introduced into the system as a result of man's rebellious nature and his paying heed to his lower desires and urges and allowing these urges and desires to override what his reason tells him. The firmware updates can also be necessitated for positive reasons, such as the case when changes in man's own spiritual state due to his spiritual growth increase mankind's capacity to receive a greater portion of God's grace. Now let us pause to consider this, as it is a very important

13. Logos and the Light of the Eye

matter. The Quran, as well as the Shi'a *hadīth*[2] report corpus, tell us that what we think of as human intelligence: our ability to speak, to understand speech and to be understood, and hence our ability to reason, is not something that was learned gradually in time through a process of intellectual and cultural evolution, contrary to what is commonly believed nowadays, in the modern and post-modern eras of ignorance. No. All such knowledge was instilled into the heart of Adam, the first human being (we do not comment on this issue with respect to Neanderthal man, or earlier pre-human creations), who then taught this primordial Adamic knowledge to Eve and to their progeny, who passed this sacred, revealed knowledge that differentiates us from the rest of the orders of creation, to their progeny, which is how it has reached us, this current generation of their offspring. This might come as a shocking revelation to some of you. "What?!" I hear you scoff. "I had heard of country bumpkins and Old Believers who deny *physical* evolution, but am I to understand that the Archer is now saying that there is no such thing as *intellectual and cultural* evolution???"

That is *exactly* what I am saying. And the empirical proof of our position is that, should any interruption in the transmission of this sacred knowledge occur, the generation that follows which is deprived of and is no longer privy to this sacred, revealed knowledge, will not be able to speak a single word of any language, which would not have been the case had this knowledge "evolved" as is commonly believed.

The Lord of the Flies

What we hope to accomplish in this section is a definitive repudiation of the possibility of the evolution of sapiential knowledge absent revelation. I remember the first time I met Michael Jones. It was in the lobby of the Āzādī Hotel in Tehran, back in 2012 or 2013. We had started a brief correspondence by email a little earlier, and I was looking forward to meeting him and talking to him in person. I had expressed an interest in his magnum opus which had just been printed, *The Jewish Revolutionary Spirit*, and he was kind enough to bring me a copy. It is such a large volume (1,200 pages), that when he gave me a copy, he said, "Here, this is the book that you can't pick up." I was a

---

[2] Hadīth: An authoritative report of a saying or deed of one of the Fourteen Immaculates (the Prophet or one of the Imāms or Lady Fātema.)

little slow on the take, so he explained amicably, "As opposed to the book that you can't put down." And that brought a smile to my face. We then went and met Mark Weber, who was another one of the invitees to the New Horizon Conference, and had several conversations regarding the Jewish Question, Tradition and Modernity, and other topics, which were recorded, and my notes which can be found in an essay in another volume. But in any event, I distinctly remember that on that first day, the conversation turned to something or other which occasioned Michael to tell me that "There is no one more conservative than I am." And I remember smiling on the inside, because this was Michael's first of many trips to Iran, and it was obvious to me that Michael had a lot to learn about what it means to be "conservative". That year, Michael and I, along with my good friend and fellow Moslem Kevin Barrett, went on a trip to Qom together, where we had a conversation with my *Ostād* (master), Magister Mahdī Nasīrī. Last month, when I saw Michael and Kevin again, this time in Mashhad, Michael and I had another conversation with Magister Nasīrī (where I acted mostly as moderator and translator), where we discussed this very issue. Michael had told me that he was writing a book on "the History of Logos and the Logos of History" (he had been reading Hegel recently), and wanted to write a chapter on the Islamic take on *logos*. And so I thought that it was only my friend and master, Magister Nasīrī, who could set him straight.

As a result of that conversation, it became apparent that while we both denied Darwin's bizarre claim that the human form and species as we now know it evolved by "chance" (the natural selection of random mutations, yada yada yada); that whereas we both denied *physical* evolution, Michael believed that the ability to speak, the "acquisition" of language, and the knowledge of how to live life as a human being "evolved" gradually over a period of time. We did not discuss how long this period was, but it was bound to be somewhere between 12,000 years (which is approximately where we Shi'a place the milestone for the creation of Adam and Eve, give or take a thousand or two), and 6,000 years ago, which is the figure most "fundamentalist" Christians believe to be the time when Adam and Eve were created (based on erroneous Biblical information).[3]

---

3   See Maurice Bucaille's *The Bible, The Quran, and Science*. Another much more significant error of the human accretions which have crept into the Jewish and Christian scripture through the ages is that Christians who at least believe the letter of the Bible (who at least believe, for example, that when the Bible says that sodomy is "an abomination"

13. Logos and the Light of the Eye

Magister Nasīrī started by going straight to the point. He put the question to Michael: What would happen if a child was separated from his parents at birth and was provided food and shelter, but had no intellectual interaction with any human being whatsoever? Would he learn language on his own? We know the answer to this to be negative, not just because it is intuitively obvious, but because there have been cases where children have indeed been separated by some freak happenstance, and somehow survived the wild, being aided by wild animals who adopted them perhaps. Such children, which are referred to as "feral" children in the literature, do not, of course, learn any human language. When Michael accepted that but said that this would not be the case if there were to be more than one child, and sufficient time was provided, Magister Nasīrī then said, ok, just think of a bunch of kids, six or seven year olds, ten year olds, even, who *can* speak! Will *they* ever "evolve" out of a state of "nature" to become civilized [and to develop a civilization which can produce, say, the *Encyclopedia Britannica*]? This is where the conversation hit an impasse and could not progress any further. Michael's position that the ability to speak, the "acquisition" of language, and the knowledge of how to live life as human beings "evolved" gradually over a period of time implied that the answer to this was affirmative. The secular humanist swill of cultural anthropology and sociology, in other words. But common sense and empirical data tell us otherwise. At this point, the conversation ended and Magister Nasīrī quipped that if Michael does not believe that these children will not "evolve" but will degenerate, [as masterfully depicted by William Golding in his 1954 novel *The Lord of the Flies*], then, not to worry, as most of the philosophers and theologians in Iran agreed with him (Michael).

So it is interesting, isn't it, that within the camp of those who deny physical evolution and believe mankind to have been created out of "clay" a few thousand years ago, that there are those who believe that the ability to speak and to understand speech, and therefore, the

---

believe it actually to be an abomination, and do not campaign for the "right" of people to sodomize each other. Good grief.) In any event, Christians believe that this 6,000 year date is not just the date for the creation of mankind, but is the date of the creation of the world itself. Well, at least they believe in it, and in the whole of it, rather than picking and choosing, or deciding that this can't be right, and that can't be right, so the whole thing must only be taken "as literature". That, (the liberal position) is decidedly more pitiable, to our mind.

ability to reason at high levels of abstraction, is something that was taught to us by God (and which cannot be acquired in any other way); whereas there are others within this large camp who believe that the ability to speak and comprehend language and to reason at high levels of abstraction, and to come up with all of the knowledge necessary to write the Encyclopedia Britannica, "just happened" in a matter of a few thousand years.

So there are two sides to this camp, one which denies the possibility of intellectual and cultural evolution, and one which avers and asserts it (while *both* deny the possibility of *physical* evolution). And there is a story or novel that represents the views of each camp. The first one we have mentioned already. It is *The Lord of the Flies*, written by William Golding and first published in 1954. It is a novel that is set during an unnamed time of war, when a plane carrying a group of British schoolboys is shot down over the Pacific. The pilot of the plane is killed, but many of the boys survive the crash and find themselves deserted on an uninhabited island, where they are alone and without adult supervision. The book portrays their disastrous attempt to govern themselves and their descent into savagery; left to themselves on a paradisiacal island, far from any civilization, the well-educated children regress to a barbaric state.

This synopsis was taken from Wikipedia or Cliff Notes or some such site, where the ending reads "left to themselves on a paradisiacal island, far from modern civilization, the well-educated children regress to a *primitive* state." I felt the need to change the word 'primitive' to 'barbaric', for while the first definition of the word 'primitive' is given as "Of or relating to an early or *original* stage or state; primeval" by *Collins* as well as the *American Heritage Dictionary,* the second definition given by both is more dominant nowadays, and especially in the context and as used in the sentence: "Occurring in or characteristic of an *early stage of development* or *evolution*". (The emphases are mine, of course.) And this is precisely the point, isn't it: do the boys regress to a primitive state (in the sense of a primeval, original state), or a barbaric one? – which, *we* argue, is not at all what our primeval, original state was like. And science and the empirical evidence is on our side; true science, as always, is on the same side as true scripture and revelation. How can it possibly be otherwise?

13. Logos and the Light of the Eye

Hayy eben Yaqzān or *Intelligentia ex Nihilo*

It is only when people don't agree with the ordinances and commandments and prohibitions of revelation and scripture that they decide to meddle with it and change it. And while the Quran, being the Final Testament, is immune to distortions and falsification, there remain, nevertheless, people within the Islamicate civilization who want to believe something other than that which it tells them; who want to believe that mankind does not stand in need of prophets, and can attain to the highest stages of knowledge and human intellectual achievement by the application of the human mind and without having any need of the faculty and institution of prophethood and revelation. Humanists, in other words. The kinds of people with this type of mentality were deeply influenced by Greek philosophy, and were happier to go about philosophizing in their merry way without the interference of Meccan and Medinan revelations. And so, back in the 12th century of the Christian era, Ibn Tufayl who was one of the philosophers among this crowd of malcontents decided to write a little story to justify the hyper-rational rants of his and of his fellow philosophers. The gist of the story was that man indeed did not stand in need of prophets and revelation, as he could and would attain to all of the highest of the transcendent wisdoms, including knowledge of God, without prophetic interference.

And of course who but Henry Corbin, philosopher *extraordinaire*, was destined to discover the manuscript of a Persian translation of and commentary on Avicenna's *Hayy ibn Yaqzān*, written in Arabic, in an Istanbul library? This discovery led him to an analysis of three of Avicenna's mystical "recitals", which were printed as *Avicenna and the Visionary Recitals* in English (by, you guessed it, our editor friends at the Princeton/ Bollingen Mythos Series in World Mythology). But more to the point, in the introduction to *The History of Hayy Ibn Yaqzān* A. S. Fulton tells us that "the Arabic philosophical fable Hayy Ibn *Yaqzān* is a classic of medieval Islamic philosophy. *Hayy Ibn Yaqzān* literally means "the Alive, son of the Awake". Ibn Tufayl (d. 1185), the Andalusian philosopher, tells the story of a child raised by a doe on an equatorial island who grows up to discover the truth about the world and his own place in it, unaided—but also unimpeded—by society, language, or tradition. His *innate intelligence*, feeble at first, develops by degrees, until it enables him to dominate his brute companions. He reaches manhood, and by ceaseless observation and reflection [!] gradually acquires a knowledge of the physical universe. Thence he advances into the realm of metaphysics and proves for himself the existence of an all-powerful Creator. Practicing ascetic discipline of mind and body he seeks for union with this One Eternal Spirit. At last he comes to the state of ecstasy, and overleaping the final metaphysical barrier, his intellect merges with the Active Intellect and he apprehends those things which eye hath not seen nor ear heard. Thus at the end of seven times seven years, *without prophet or revelation* (the emphasis is mine), he achieves the utmost fullness of knowledge and ineffable felicity in mystical union with his Lord".[4] You can't make this stuff up, and you can't stop stupid.

So Ibn Tufayl, representing the secular humanist cultural anthropologist contingent, avers that it was Hayy eben Yaqzān's *innate intelligence* unaided by prophet or revelation which took him to the lofty intellectual and spiritual stations of what is referred to nowadays as the "Transcendental Wisdom" (*Hekmat-e Mote'ālīeh* – after Mollā Sadra's philosophic synthesis). And yet, in an essay which appeared in *Nouvelle* École shortly before his passing entitled "Entretien avec Konrad Lorenz", we see the conservative German philosopher, sociologist, and anthropologist Arnold Gehlen asserting that "Virtually every conscious realm of human activity comes to be affected by culture. In his anthropology, it is virtually inseparable from man. For without it, and the role it plays in negotiating man's encounters with the world, man would be only an undifferentiated and still unrealizable facet of nature — unable, in fact, to survive in nature."[5] Alain de Benoist correctly comments with regards to this assertion that "Contrary to a long tradition of rationalist thought (the anthropological structuralism of Claude Lévi-Strauss being the foremost recent example), there is no "natural man." Free of culture, *man would be a cretin, unable even to speak*".[6]

What is highly interesting to me personally regarding the juxtaposition of these two stories is that one is written by a Moslem thinker before

---

4 From A. S. Fulton's Introduction in *The History of Hayy Ibn Yaqzan* by Abu Bakr ibn at-Tufayl; translated from the Arabic by Simon Ockley; revised, with an Introduction by A. S. Fulton.

5 *Nouvelle École* 25-26 (Winter 1975-6).

6 Quoted in Michael O'Meara, *New Culture, New Right: Anti-Liberalism in Postmodern Europe*, Arktos Media, 2013; pages 66-67.

13. Logos and the Light of the Eye

the Mongol Invasion in the High Middle Ages, who gets it completely wrong, and the other is written by an atheist modern in the late stages of Modernity, who gets it absolutely right. What is also interesting is that I remember reading an interview with Mr. Golding many moons ago (so I cannot cite the source) where he made an interesting comment about this book of his. In response to the question posed to him concerning the ship that arrives at the end of the book which saved the children who had "reverted" to barbarism, he said that the book was about the condition of mankind, but that he was not as optimistic as the ending of the book, "as no one is coming". Well, he didn't get it *all* right. The Universal Savior, the Imam al-Mahdi's return is a divinely-guaranteed certainty, and he will be preceded by the Second Coming of the Christ Jesus, son of Lady Mary. But if the book is, as he says, a parable for the state of humanity and how it has degenerated from an original state of grace to one of barbarism, then he has certainly gotten that part of it right, and for that we offer him our thanks and prayers, and trust that the Most Merciful will have mercy on his tortured soul. Amen.

"The Word" between Athens and Jerusalem

If we take the translation of logos as "the word", as in, "In the beginning was the Word"[7], and we recall what we stated earlier which was that the distinction between reason and revelation was an artificial one, and that it was all revelation, the first one being an initial revelation where God "Taught Adam all the Names" (which we likened to the "firmware" that is installed on a given computer system), and the second one being the various revelations which were revealed to humanity throughout our history by way of the prophets (which can be likened to "software" and so many software updates), then the implication is that two things can go wrong. The first is that the firmware can be erased, as in the case of *The Lord of the Flies*, or not installed at all by the parents, as in the case of children deprived of being taught the grace of the knowledge of "All the names" and language, which are referred to as "feral" children raised by wild animals or "wild" children.[8] The second is that the software can be

---

7 John 1:1: In the beginning was "the Word", (a translation of the Greek word "Logos").

8 See the Excursus at the end of this chapter for a fascinating glimpse into what happens when children are left to their own devices and are blind to the guidance of revelation

erased or, as is more common, corrupted, so that while people have language skills (the firmware), they do not have the proper software to run on it, because the software that was revealed by God in order to guide mankind and to teach us how to live a life of moral virtue and righteousness has been corrupted by human interference:

أُمِرُوا إِلَّا لِيَعْبُدُوا إِلَٰهًا وَاحِدًا لَّا إِلَٰهَ إِلَّا هُوَ سُبْحَانَهُ عَمَّا يُشْرِكُونَاتَّخَذُوا أَحْبَارَهُمْ وَرُهْبَانَهُمْ أَرْبَابًا مِّن دُونِ اللَّهِ وَالْمَسِيحَ ابْنَ مَرْيَمَ وَمَا

[9:31] They have taken their rabbis and their monks – as well as the Christ, son of Mary – for their lords beside God, although they had been bidden to worship none but the One God, save whom there is no deity: the One who is utterly remote, in His limitless glory, from anything to which they may ascribe a share in His divinity!

And this is why God, in His infinite grace, continued to commission prophets and send them to mankind. And this is also the reason why, being the Final Testament, the Quran will be kept by God to be immune from distortion and falsification:

إِنَّا نَحْنُ نَزَّلْنَا الذِّكْرَ وَإِنَّا لَهُ لَحَافِظُونَ

[15:9] Behold, it is We Ourselves who have bestowed from on high, step by step, this reminder. And, behold, it is We who will assuredly guard it [from all corruption].

Another important implication of this conceptualization of logos as "the Word" and as the imparting unto Adam the names of all things per 2:31 of the Quran, is that the distinction between reason and revelation, or between Athens and Jerusalem, fades away. The question of the compatibility or incompatibility between reason and religion was one of the main points of contention in the Middle Ages, followed by the issue of the relationship between religion and science; both of which were important issues which the Catholic Church had to contend with at the time. The dichotomies that plagued the west in the Middle Ages such

---

and language and the knowledge that was imparted to the progenitor of the human race, the prophet Adam, unto whom be God's peace.

as the conflict between religion and science, and the conflict between religion and reason, never obtained in Islam, and Moslems are at a loss to understand what these supposed conflicts mean. One of the criteria for arriving at the creedal beliefs and primary and derivative laws in Islam is reason (in addition to the other three sources of the Quran, the *hadīth* report corpus, and magisterial or scholarly consensus). Furthermore, and most importantly, one cannot attain to faith in the creedal beliefs of Islam by reference to or reliance upon scriptural sources (i.e. the Quran and the *hadīth* report corpus), as these become sources for the derivation of correct belief and law only *after* one has attained to faith in Islam. For the act of attaining to faith, both the Quran and the magisterium of Islam say that one must use his or her reason and can *only* use his or her reason. This makes sense, by the way, as one cannot attain to faith in something in any other way: one cannot force oneself to believe something if one's reason is not convinced of it, even if one's life depended on it. Once one attains to faith in Islam by virtue of the pure force of reason and the rational arguments in its favor (note that there is no irrationalist Kierkegaardian "leap of faith" here), then he or she can use Islam's scriptural sources for attaining to faith in Islam's secondary beliefs and for the derivation of law (provided that one is so qualified). Thus, reason is given a very high station in Islam and its use is logically prior to the use of its scripture. (Of course, there are many rational arguments *within* the scripture, and within the Quran in particular, and there is no obstacle to referring to these arguments in order to determine the veracity of the faith.)

Pre-Ontological Chaos

At their deepest level, Dugin's Heideggerian critique and de Benoist's Nietzschean critique of liberalism and modernity do away with what has been described as the idea of a universal prescription, such as came with "the Christian's alien logos", their "dogmatic assertions" and their "either/or logic". But as we explained above, according to our understanding, *logos* is the light that God revealed in order for us to be able to grow spiritually, to perfect ourselves in a journey that began with Him and which will end up with us returning back to him ([2:156] *"Verily, unto God do we belong and, verily, unto Him we shall be returned"*), and to aspire to be worthy of the Burden of the

The European New Right - A Shia Response

Trust that we took on at the Day of Alast[9], and to aspire to become His vicegerent on Earth. It is the lantern that God has given us as a grace to accompany each of us on our journeys back to Him. In order to take a glimpse at just how dark this journey is, we again invite the gentle reader to read some of the horrifying stories that we have gleaned from a BBC article on what they call "feral" children, but what are in fact nothing less than children who have been deprived of their God-given right to the lantern of revelation.

If you want an "alternative logos" (Dugin), then, to the best of my knowledge, the options are, switching the light off and "going to the dark side" (it seems there is good reason for the expression); or, secular humanism, polytheism, pantheism, atheism, and all of the other isms that a philosophical approach to life is happy to provide. Logos is the ability to speak, and so, if you want to get an idea of what an "alternative logos" looks like, we respectfully refer you to the Excursus at the end of this chapter where you will be able to read about the unfortunate souls who have indeed been deprived of logos, and the miserable state of "pre-ontological chaos" that they were transmogrified into.

Without the Light of Logos having been revealed, Hayy b. Yaqzan would be a mute, not a wise sage who is not in need of prophethood and revelation. And without the ship coming to save the children in *The Lord of the Flies*, they would have destroyed themselves as surely as we have all but destroyed the planet which was given to us in trust, and as surely as we will destroy ourselves, if not with nuclear or biological weapons, with GMO's, artificial intelligence and/or transhumanism, whichever comes first.

So given the metaphor for logos that we prefer, we thus reject the following characterization of logos by Alexander Dugin as being the Yin to chaos' Yang:

> Logos itself cannot exist without chaos, like fish cannot live without water. When we take a fish out of water, it dies. When the fish begins to insist excessively that there is something other than water around it, even if it is true, it comes to the shore and

---

9   See *Creedal Foundations of Walīyic Islam*, Chapter 2, Section 2.5.

13. Logos and the Light of the Eye

dies there. It is a kind of mad fish. When we put it back in the water, it only jumps out again. So, let it die this way if it wants. There are other fishes deep in the water. Let us follow them.

But there are no other fish in the depths. Even anatomically, the Yin is 1 and the Yang is 0. And zero is zero, no matter how you slice and dice it. Even within Dugin's metaphor, Yin is the 'ground of being' (Tillich?) and thus can never be being itself. But to revert back to the metaphor which we prefer, what we say, rather, is that Dugin and de Benoist want to pluck out the Eye of Logic and throw it out (one in favor of some pre-rational oceanic polyvalent state and the other in favor of some "pre-ontological chaos",[10] whatever that might be – the question is left completely open), whereas what needs to be done, which is Islam's prescription, is to take modernity's and the Enlightenment's Eye of Logic which is pointed *downward* toward the material world and all things that are tangible and quantifiable, and change its *direction* so that it is pointing heavenward, so that the dead end that this erroneous direction engenders is overcome first by bringing the entire horizon into view, and then, moving upwards even more, enabling the whole of the heavens above to be taken in with eyes wide open. And before too long, given sufficient humility before the Creator, one's *Third* Eye will even open, by the grace of God, so that one can see *into* the heavens, into higher states of being (*samāwāt*), into states of reality which are more real than that of this material plane's, which is the lowest possible state of existence (*asfal as-sāfelīn*).

لَقَدْ خَلَقْنَا الْإِنسَانَ فِي أَحْسَنِ تَقْوِيمٍ

ثُمَّ رَدَدْنَاهُ أَسْفَلَ سَافِلِينَ

[95:4] Verily, We create man in the finest of forms; [95:5] and then We relegated him to the lowest of the low [orders of being].

From our perspective, these kinds of returns to prerational pantheistic nowheres and Heideggerian wholesale rejections of multi-millennial traditions for the sake of saving tradition are first and foremost unnecessary (as superior and logically tenable alternatives exist in

---

10 "... We should appeal to chaos in its original Greek sense, as to something that precedes being and order, something pre-ontological."

The European New Right - A Shia Response

Shi'a Islam); and secondly, such efforts come about as a result of not being aware of a viable alternative to provide a handhold out of the modernist nightmare, and do not have any appeal in and of themselves, i.e. they are essentially unattractive or unattractive in their essence – both logically, as well as aesthetically and spiritually (they do not resonate with one's innate primordial disposition). And of course, most importantly, neither alternative provides a comprehensive, integral, positive program; they are both only at the stage of negative criticism, and, unlike Shi'a Islam, have nothing positive to add that is substantive.

The issue of chaos proposed as an alternative to logos is a case in point. Brother Alexander riles against "the exclusivist principle called logos" and says that it has "expired and we all will be buried under its ruins unless we make an appeal to chaos and its metaphysical principles". Brother Alexander cautions that we need to distinguish between two kinds of chaos: "the postmodernist 'chaos' as an equivalent to confusion, a kind of post-order, and the Greek chaos as pre-order, as something that exists before ordered reality has come into being. Only the latter can be considered as chaos in the proper sense of the word."

He then goes on to say that "chaos is something opposite to logos, its absolute alternative." But as we have seen, *chaos* is a category made possible by the latitude afforded by *logos* and by way of the *nóos*. Chaos is not an alternative to logos. It is not even the absence of logos. It is denatured logos; corrupted logos. If we liken the world to a TV screen, then chaos would not be the black and white flickering light (sometimes called "noise" or "white noise") that we get when there is no signal. Chaos is the lewd and violent Satanic shit that is churned out of Hollywood and piped into Iranian airspace against our vocal protestations to no effect by upwards of 200 satellite channels mostly paid for by CIA covert funds, but many of them also creeping out of that cesspool that is known as London (courtesy of funding provided by Her Majesty's Wahhabeast client states in the Persian Gulf and Arabia) because we refuse to hand over ownership of our central bank and our power to generate our own money to the "Jewish" cabal that runs the City of London (with their so-called Christian and Moslem collaborationists, of course – let us be clear about that). And so, chaos is no alternative at all, be it ontological or "pre-ontological". All you have to do is to read the few lines in the following Excursus to see what the face of chaos looks like.

13. Logos and the Light of the Eye

Excursus: Children Deprived of Revelation

When children are separated from their parents at a young age, they are deprived of the opportunity to partake of the intelligence which was imparted by God unto the prophets, who in turn taught this knowledge and wisdom to humanity. These kinds of children are called "Feral" Children[11] in the literature, and a glimpse into what happens to them in the absence of revealed knowledge demonstrates how deeply dependent we as human beings are on the knowledge that was revealed by God for our benefit.

1. "Oxana was found living with dogs in a kennel in 1991. She was eight years old and had lived with the dogs for six years. Her parents were alcoholics and one night, they had left her outside. Looking for warmth, the three-year-old crawled into the farm kennel and curled up with the mongrel dogs, an act that probably saved her life. *She ran on all fours, panted with her tongue out, bared her teeth and barked.* Because of her lack of human interaction, she only knew the words 'yes' and 'no'."

2. "Marina Chapman was kidnapped in 1954 at five years of age from a remote South American village and left by her kidnappers in the jungle," says Fullerton-Batten. "She lived with a family of capuchin monkeys for five years before she was discovered by hunters. She ate berries, roots and bananas dropped by the monkeys; slept in holes in trees and *walked on all fours, like the monkeys.* It was not as though the monkeys were giving her food – she had to learn to survive, she had the ability and common sense – she copied their behavior and they became used to her, pulling lice out of her hair and treating her like a monkey."

3. "John Ssebunya ran away from home in 1988 when he was three years old after seeing his father murder his mother," says Fullerton-Batten. "He fled into the jungle where he lived with monkeys. He was captured in 1991, now about six years old, and placed in an orphanage... *He had calluses on his knees from walking like a monkey.*"

---

[11] Excerpted from an article on bbc.com (Retrieved June 2018) (http://www.bbc.com/culture/story/20151012-feral-the-children-raised-by-wolves)

4. Madina lived with dogs from birth until she was three years old, sharing their food, playing with them, and sleeping with them when it was cold in winter. When social workers found her in 2013, *she was naked, walking on all fours and growling like a dog.*

5. Sujit was eight years old when he was found in the middle of a road clucking and flapping his arms and behaving like a chicken," says Fullerton-Batten. *"He pecked at his food, crouched on a chair as if roosting, and would make rapid clicking noises with his tongue.* His parents locked him in a chicken coop. His mother committed suicide and his father was murdered. His grandfather took responsibility for him but still kept him confined in the chicken coop." For the children, the transition after being found could be as difficult as the years spent in isolation. "When they were discovered, it was such a shock – they had learnt animal behavior, *their fingers were claw-like and they couldn't even hold a spoon."*

14. Objective Truth and Radical Postmodern Subjectivism

The Imam is Occulted (or, Shi'a Islam does not hold the key to solving the world's problems either)

One would have thought that Alexander Dugin's being an avowed Russian Orthodox Christian would have limited the discussion of the issue of ontological pluralism (and subjectivism, its epistemological corollary) to the critique of the thought of Alain de Benoist and the Grecists and the ENR who have abandoned any pretense to Christianity and its universalist logos, and who advocate something that goes back to a culture that predates the introduction of Christianity to Europe. But alas, the cogency of the critique of the post-moderns and its pluralist and subjectivist incursions on the thought of Brother Alexander mean that this is not the case.

And this is where it gets tricky, because one would expect a Shi'a critique of the thought of Alexander Dugin to harp on this obvious contradiction between his avowed Russian Orthodoxy and the error of his siding with the post-moderns' rejection of the objectivism of Aristotelianism, Augustinian theology, the Thomist synthesis of Medieval Christianity, the universalism of early modernity and the Enlightenment thinkers, and of Islam generally. I say a Shi'a critique, and by that I mean one that actually represents the millennial tradition of Shi'a Islam, and not the so-called philosophical-mystical "Shi'aism" represented by Henry Corbin, or the Perennialist "Shi'aism" of Seyyed Hossein Nasr's supposed "traditionalist" perspective, or the secular/orientalist extraordinaire "Shi'aism" of Mohammad Ali Amir-Moezzi, for that matter – none of which would have any problems with the "openness" of Brother Dugin's pluralism and would welcome it with open arms. And, to be sure, there is not a uniform voice on this issue within the *actual* millennial tradition of Shi'a Islam either, which, if our *olamā* (religious scholars) bothered themselves to learn a single word of English and to actually engage the world outside their comfortably numb collective cocoon, the gentle reader would have been able to acquaint him or herself with what they had to say,

The European New Right - A Shia Response

instead of relying on the questionable skills of this, your lowly and wretched interlocutor and interpreter. And the absence of consensus is, I would venture to aver, a symptom of what we call the condition of the End Times, and what those who are more sophisticated than us Old Believers would call a symptom of post-modernity.

And yes, we *do* point out the contradiction, but we do not harp on it or dwell on it to excess. The profanation process of the secular humanism of the Renaissance, which saw its culmination in the Reformation and the Enlightenment (the "Second Reformation" as the late great Christopher Dawson used to call it) unleashed the Ouroboros serpent of modernity which consumed the civilization of the West by eating its own tail. As a result, in their bewilderment, there are those Catholics like my friends Mike Jones and Bishop Richard Williamson (as well as Christopher Dawson himself) who hold fast to the pre-modern position (and deal with the whole fiasco whose symptom manifested itself in the Second Vatican Council, each in their own unique ways). And there are those, like my friend Alexander Dugin, who, despite their Orthodox faith, err on the side of the pluralism of post-modernity, and somehow reconcile this with their faith in ways that are not clear to me.

Now within our tradition, it not having matriculated to the fraternity of those whose self-doubt has crippled them, our issue is not whether or not we can be sure that what we believe is true (and whether our whole civilizational journey was nothing but a wet dream). Rather, the central question in the spectrum within Shi'a Islam in the past half century concerns the advisability of the *olamā* taking a leading role in rising in insurrection against the illegitimate government of the day in order to establish an Islamic constitutional order. The Hojjatieh Society and its intellectual offshoots can be seen on one end of this spectrum, headed by Sheikh Mahmoud Tavallāī better known as Halabī (1900 - 1998), whose position concerning rising in insurrection to form an Islamic government is that, on the basis of *hadīth* reports from the Shi'a *hadīth* corpus, no action whatsoever in this regard is permissible until the advent of the occulted twelfth Imam, the *Sāheb oz-Zamān* or Lord of the Age. On the other end of the spectrum, of course, is the now well-known position of Imam Khomeini (1902 - 1989), a near contemporary of Shaykh Halabī, and his students, the best known of which are Ayatollahs Montazerī, Beheshtī, Khāmeneī, Rafsanjānī, Javādī-e Āmolī, Makārem-e Shīrāzī, Sobhānī, and so on. These scholars of religion believe not only that

14. Objective Truth and Radical Postmodern Subjectivism

religious scholars *may* rise in insurrection against illegitimate (*tāghūt*) regimes, but indeed have a religious *duty* to do so; and furthermore, that they are empowered to act absolutely in all matters of state (as well as in all religio-juridical matters, of course). We do not mean to imply that the ideology of this group was or is such that they believe that they were or are capable of realizing a constitutional order that is able to implement one hundred percent of the ordinances and values and ideals of Islam. But all of them do believe that they are able to implement an order that reflects an Islam that is something between, say, seventy to ninety percent of that which the Prophet and the Imams had in mind. The middle position is that which is occupied by the likes of Ayatollahs Vahīd-e Khorāsānī, Mīrzā Javād-e Tabrīzī, Khoī, and Sistani, who believe that there are insufficient scriptural bases for a compelling case of there being a duty for the *olamā* to rise up in insurrection and to form an Islamic order, but at the same time, they believe that the *olamā* have been given wide-ranging authority on the basis of the portal or opening of expediency (*bāb-e hesba*), and further hold (contra the Hojjatieh) that it is not permissible to take a position *against* those among their fellow *olamā* who believe it is incumbent on them to rise up in insurrection (*"valī mokhālefat rā jā'ez nemīdānand"*), or against those who have succeeded in doing so in Iran.

Not that it matters, but my own position favors that of Imam Khomeinī, with the important proviso that they are aiming too high, and that what we should hope to achieve is not a 90% or even a 70% Islam, but one that is closer to the 30% mark, God willing; and that given the fact that the Era of Occultation has reached a critical point, where the very bindings of society and understanding and comprehension itself have begun to unravel, our task is almost a Sisyphusian one, except that contra William Golding who stated that he did not believe that a ship was coming to save the children of his creation on the Island of *The Lord of the Flies*, a Universal Savior is indeed expected, and it will not be too long before his blessed advent. I mention my own position simply in order to elucidate the fact that because I do not believe that we, being the small minority community within humanity known as Shi'a Islam, have the answers or the keys to solve the world's problems, that therefore, we are sympathetic to those of our fellow brothers and sisters in the Family of Man who are struggling for the cause of social justice, but who happen to have inconsistencies and contradictions other than those which we suffer from. And that is why, while we might point out a contradiction and even a basic contradiction in the thought of our friends and comrades in arms, we do so in what we hope is a cordial spirit and one which we pray and trust is constructive.

Thus, we believe that the post-modern critique of Western modernity serves a good purpose in so far as it makes the West aware of its errors, but does no one any good when it does away with the whole Western intellectual tradition root and branch a la Nietzsche, Kierkegaard and Heidegger; and we would caution our friends to stay away from such wholesale destruction unless and until they are also accompanied by *positive* integral replacements. And this is because it is easy to piss in the wind, but as those Neocon bastards keep finding out (yet never learn, being the morons that they are), you have to watch out for something called blowback, or else, like the Neocons, you will show up at the party with your pants all wet in the front and all down the legs.

And so, when Brother Alexander, agreeing with Heidegger that logos *itself* has to be jettisoned, and says that "Instead of the ideas of the monotonic process, progress, and modernization, we must endorse other slogans directed toward life, repetition, the preservation of that which is of value and changing that which should be changed"; what we say is, fine, but preserving "that which is of value" and changing "that which should be changed" based on what criteria? Where is *your* magisterium?? An oceanic yearning for a "pre-ontological" chaos (as opposed to the post-modern one) is not sufficient. That was tried by Molla Sadra (d. 1636), who is characterized by the Stanford Encyclopedia of Philosophy as being "arguably the most significant Islamic philosopher after Avicenna". Molla Sadra is said to have "championed a radical philosophical method that attempted to transcend the simple dichotomy between a discursive, ratiocinative mode of reasoning and knowing, and a more intuitive, poetic and non-propositional mode of knowledge." So the idea of going beyond logos and back to a "pre-ontological" chaos has already been attempted. But he chumped out like all the other philosophers who came before him and went after him, because he did not understand the first principle of Islam, *towhīd*, as explicated by the Imams, so that the whole edifice of his metaphysical system was built on a cornerstone which is undermined by the metaphysical reality which we tried to elucidate in the Proof of Finitude in one of the early sections above.

14. Objective Truth and Radical Postmodern Subjectivism

The Logical Impossibility of a Non-Foundationalist Paradigm

The "exclusivism" of the Christian logos and the "universalism" of the enlightenment and liberalism are bemoaned by post-moderns. But they have yet to solve the logical contradiction that by excluding an exclusivist position, one is being exclusivist oneself; or that if one is against universalism, one is either against it locally, or universally; and that if one is against it locally, then one leaves room for it; whereas if one is against it universally, one is being universalist oneself. And of course the reason they have yet to solve this contradiction is that it is unsolvable without positing a solution, by which is meant a solution that stands up to scrutiny or a "solid" solution, by which is meant one that has a foundation, by which is meant a foundationalist solution, which of course undermines their original intention. The "problem" of foundationalism is in-built to the structure of language itself; it is *syntactically* impossible to get away from it. By stating that "Nothing is true (in an objective or foundational sense)", you are at one and the same time making the objective assertion that something *is* true (in an objective or foundational sense), namely, "nothing". And so on. Thus, we are back to square one, which is that we must start with laying down real and objectively held first principles as the cornerstones and foundations of any system which we care to build.

Michael O'Meara tells us that "Postmodernists conclude that there are no cognitively privileged and canonical forms of knowledge — only different styles, voices, and registers reflecting different perspectives, different premises, and different systems of symbolization;"[1] and that "postmodernity collapses the universal into the particular, the global into the local, the objective into the subjective." He then goes on to state that although "[the] Grécistes acknowledge that "truth" is an interpretative product of a particular tradition (that is, anti-foundational), they also believe that this does not imply, as postmodernists assume, that "truth" is entirely free-floating, that any "truth" can be embraced by any subject, or that empirical reality can bend to any subjective intent. Against a bourgeois/academic postmodernity committed to the nihilistic "reconstructionism" of modern liberal politics, Grécistes argue that "truth" is a function

---

1 Michael O'Meara, *New Culture, New Right: Anti-Liberalism in Postmodern Europe*, Arktos Media, 2013.

of culture and history, "authorized" by context alone — a context, moreover, that is never arbitrary, but lived, felt, rooted."[2]

Let us give full credit here to Michael O'Meara for making the fine distinction, but we would respectfully suggest that this is an act of sophistry and a clutching at straws on the part of the Grécistes. You either have a solid foundation to build upon, or you don't. And if you don't, you can clutch at straws all day long, but they will go down with you when you drown and will not be capable of providing you with any kind of intellectual footing. The Grécistes would do well to recognize that the abandonment of the absolute criteria which are provided by revelation but were characterized as "tales of the ancients" by the Enlightenment thinkers was the beginning of nihilism in the West and not "humanity's" coming of age. As Michael O'Meara astutely observes again, once such absolute criteria are abandoned, "representations of all kinds are inevitably entwined in sociolinguistic webs of signification that know no all-embracing truth, only their own truths, which are indistinguishable from their will to power... [and break down and degenerate into] a self-conscious throng of incompatible discursive traditions."[3]

And so here again we have a tale of unintended consequences or blowback: "The Reformers' greatest success came, ironically, not in re-ordering Christian spiritual life, but in setting off a process that would undermine the authority of Christianity in any of its forms, for in challenging the established Church they inadvertently let loose the forces of skepticism and secularism, relativism and tolerance [without constraint] — as "objective revelation" was supplanted by practical ethico-religious subjectivities."[4]

What the Reformers failed to bear in mind, as did the Enlightenment thinkers who followed in their wake, is that if no statement has any objective validity, then any statement that asserts this has none either. And if you take this same logic and apply it at the macro level, it will look like this: If a culture cannot be judged by anything other than its own values, then no culture has a right to judge any other culture

---

2   Ibid.
3   Ibid.
4   Ibid.

14. Objective Truth and Radical Postmodern Subjectivism

and no one has a right to judge anyone else (and so then, why are you judging the liberal culture who wants to take over the whole world; after all, a shark is a shark, and if it wants to eat all the fish in the sea, then who are we to judge them for what they do?) This is the exact trap of cultural pluralism which the Perennialist have fallen into (of which we will speak more in the section which follows), dragging Alexander Dugin and the European New Right right along with them. To wit, one cannot maintain with the postmodernists, based on their radical subjectivist epistemology, that the values and practices of every culture cannot be judged objectively as "everything is relative" (an absolute statement) and that sexuality and gender identity, for example, are therefore nothing but "social constructs" which have no metaphysical and moral reality, and then turn around and bemoan, with the Perennialists (but contra the postmoderns, who are at least consistent), the fact that sexuality and gender identity are nothing but social constructs which have no metaphysical and moral reality (which is why the whole traditional edifice of gender identity and roles and sexual boundaries has come tumbling down in the West).

Thus the radical pluralism of the postmodernists that "deconstructs" modernist notions of truth, value, and justice in the interests of "a wider field of localized representations and practices" does not stand up to the sword of their own radical reason, as each of these "localized representations and practices" must themselves be based on solid objective and universally applicable foundations. This is not something that is escapable: each cultural pole by definition must assert itself as being preferable to other cultures, unless it is amorphous in which case it is not a culture or a pole and does not merit our consideration as it will resolve itself and be assimilated into its neighboring poles. So no, the assertions of different notions of truth, value, and justice cannot be overcome, nor can their universal applicability be overcome. But what *can* and must be overcome is the outrageous desire to want to impose such notions on others *by coercion and force*. Thus, rather than the collapse of the metanarrative leading to an absurdist refusal of "the tyranny of wholes" (stupidly, Ihab Hassan), what we should gain from the righteous criticisms of the post-moderns is the humility that comes from recognizing that what we believe to be true and that which we hold to be sacred in the deepest core of our hearts, does not necessarily obtain for the rest of humanity and thus will not and shall not apply to the rest of humanity unless and until portions of it come to see our truth *by way of rational and peaceful debate and discourse*. Thus, Dugin is wrong when he affirms a position that is *absolutely* subjective (see what I mean when I say that subjectivism is syntactically impossible?):

> "Societies can be compared, but we cannot state that any one of them is objectively better than the others. Such an assessment is always subjective, and any attempt to raise a subjective assessment to the status of a theory is racism. This type of an attempt is unscientific and inhumane. The differences between societies in any sense can, in no shape or form, imply the superiority of one over the other."

No, Brother Alexander. Not only is such a position logically untenable ("Everything is subjective" is an absurd position as it undermines itself, for if *everything* is subjective, then that position is also subjective and holds no water); but much more importantly – I mean, forget logic – such a position is an abandonment of the sacred and a wholesale capitulation to secularism. One cannot maintain, for example, that salvation can only be achieved through the recognition of the Christ Jesus as one's savior, and maintain at the same time that a community or society who lives in accordance with this belief and the tenets that were revealed by Jesus is not "objectively better than the others". This is a case of over-compensation which is logically both unnecessary and untenable, creedaly heretical, and an intellectual posture which desacralizes the spiritual and profanes one's soul.

Here's another example from Brother Alexander: "The differences between societies in any sense can, in no shape or form, imply the superiority of one over the other. This is a central axiom of the Fourth Political Theory." Again, this is relativistic and therefore self-undermining, because what the statement is really saying is that the differences between societies in no way imply the superiority of one over the other [with the exception of those who subscribe to this "central axiom of the Fourth Political Theory" which we are hereby positing *is* superior to the other theories, for else, why would we be bothering to posit anything at all?] On the other hand, we *do* recognize and agree with the formulation of Eurasianism if and when put in the following terms:

14. Objective Truth and Radical Postmodern Subjectivism

Eurasianism, recognizing the pretense of the Western logos to universality, refuses to recognize this universality as an inevitability. This is the specific character of Eurasianism. It considers Western culture as a local and temporary phenomenon, and affirms a multiplicity of cultures and civilisations which coexist at different moments of a cycle.[5]

How we would formulate it is that we recognize liberalism's emic universality in theory, but refuse its values, and so do not allow them within the territories of our universe, where our universal values reign supreme. We can add, furthermore, that we welcome an intellectual sparring, knowing that liberalism might win on some points, but that our ideology will ultimately prevail. O'Meara states that the early Church hoped to reorganize the world on the basis of its indisputable truths and that Liberalism would later seek to do the same, but did so by substituting "a secular concept of *logos*" for the real thing. Every social order has to have a foundational base, a rock bottom. It cannot just float in the air. And this is very basic; the most basic of levels. Thus, if the various poles of the multipolar world advocated by Alexander Dugin are not firmly grounded in absolute, objective reality, and if the Liberal Order is, then we would say that we are closer to the Liberals with respect to our metaphysics than we are to Brother Dugin. But we hasten to add, of course, that we are adamantly against liberalism's insatiable demand to impose its universalism on our territories by coercion and force. In our opinion, its universal values are unsound, and its desire to impose them on others under some stupid concocted "New World Order" are even more unsound; but the fact that they recognize that their culture and civilization must necessarily be based on universal values puts them that much ahead of those who fail to recognize this basic fact and are crippled as a consequence of this failure.

Michael O'Meara tells us that for New Rightists, "it is the difference between mythos and logos that best illustrates the spiritual divide separating the open-ended holism of ancient European paganism from Judeo-Christian dualism and its liberal offshoots." We have already talked about the logical shortcomings of a culture or system of thought which does not own to maintaining a foundational metaphysics. But

---

[5] Alexander Dugin, *The Fourth Political Theory*, Arktos Media, 2009.

let us elaborate on the spiritual aspect. We vehemently and absolutely believe that this is the bottom line (but just as vehemently and absolutely will not impose our view on others, but only hope to win others over by the force of our argument): either there *is* a single God who has a will and wants His subjects to abide by that will, and has created the world in such a way, and ordered it in such a way to have a *logos*, a divine order to which one must willingly or unwillingly submit; or there is no such thing and it is all "tales of the ancients"

ثُمَّ اسْتَوَىٰ إِلَى السَّمَاءِ وَهِيَ دُخَانٌ فَقَالَ لَهَا وَلِلْأَرْضِ ائْتِيَا طَوْعًا أَوْ كَرْهًا

قَالَتَا أَتَيْنَا طَائِعِينَ

[41:11] And He [it is who] applied His design to the skies, which were [yet but] smoke; and He [it is who] said to them and to the earth, "Come [into being], both of you, willingly or unwillingly!" – to which both responded, "We do come in obedience."

أَفَغَيْرَ دِينِ اللَّـهِ يَبْغُونَ وَلَهُ أَسْلَمَ مَن فِي السَّمَاوَاتِ وَالْأَرْضِ طَوْعًا وَكَرْهًا وَإِلَيْهِ يُرْجَعُونَ

[3:83] Do they seek, perchance, a faith other than in God, although it is unto Him that whatever is in the heavens and on earth surrenders itself, willingly or unwillingly, since unto Him all must return?

If there is no higher power, there can be no objectivity and no immutable truths. That is where it all begins: at the trans-temporal eschaton and telos to which end all of human history is being drawn, and at the first fork in the road. You cannot get away from the nihilism of modernity with its radical and crushing nihilism of no higher power, no objectivity, and no immutable truths, and most important of all, therefore, no life of bliss in ever-lasting heaven without going back to that fork and taking the other tine, the "red pill" of *al-haqq*. But because of the crooked laying of the cornerstone of the Christian Church and Pauline Christianity, and because of all of the problems

14. Objective Truth and Radical Postmodern Subjectivism

that followed in the wake of its founding, Christianity is no longer viable as that "red pill", as its "tales of the ancients" baggage is too toxic and determinative, making it a spent force. But because the majoritarian strain of Islam suffered and suffers from a fate that is similar to Christianity, that red pill cannot be Sunni Islam either. To our mind, the only rational choice left is Shi'a Islam. But when we say this, we do not in the least mean to imply that the Shi'a tradition has been immune to these problems. Not at all. We are burdened with massive problems just as you are, of all stripes and flavors. But theologically and therefore spiritually, we seem to be head and shoulders above all of the other options that are out there. But our orthodoxy is one thing, and our orthopraxy is quite another; and there, while we are certainly ahead of the West and of Christendom generally in certain respects, there is also certainly room for us to learn from you and much room for improvement.

Shi'a Islam and the Islamic Republic of Iran and the project to re-establish Islam as it was meant to be not only has its share of problems, but I would go further than that and say that this project is doomed to fail, as it has failed in practically all of the major indicators be they ethical or having to do with the establishment of social justice, with the significant but ultimately irrelevant exception of the indicator of *material* progress, in which the Islamic Republic is off the (UN Development Index) charts; but Shi'a Islam nevertheless remains closest to the truth and it is the only religion that is capable of reconciling reason with revealed truth, and thus, of integrating the affairs of religion, i.e. the moral tenets which a society holds most dear and holds as sacred, with the affairs of state, i.e. the institution which is the most powerful instrument available to a community to enshrine its sacred values into law so as to protect and foster and maintain them. But unless and until we who live in "the Besieged Shi'a Citadel" actually start to *live* (and not just to talk and write) as Shi'a Moslems, at which point the luminescence of our example will outshine the *zolomāt* darkness that is still hanging over our heads like a dark fog that won't let up; then all this talk will be for naught, as ultimately, and rightly, people do not care about the veracity of an argument no matter how forceful it is, if the supposed system that it is advocating fails to deliver the goods, which is righteous ethical behavior – an acid test, some of whose parameters we continue to fail to meet, especially when it comes to implementing social justice, but also and more simply, in our failure to hold our responsible authorities to account, and to bring about transparency and other prerequisites in the accountability infrastructure of our polity.

The False Appeal of the Perennialists

Another related error that is held in common by Brother Alexander and Brother Alain de Benoist is this cozying up to the Perennialist, be they Rene Guenon, Julius Evola, Frithjof Schuon, Martin Lings, etc. This movement has a lot of positives on offer, not least their nuanced critique of the modern and post-modern condition, and their desire to hold on to that which is sacred. But their methodological error of insisting on cultural pluralism undermines that very goal, as the sacred is, by definition, and can only be absolute. If we assert with Michael O'Meara that "postmodernity marks that stage in late modern consciousness when modernity began to recognize the subjective foundations of its own narrative projections" and to favor subjectivity over an objective epistemology and a pluralist ontology over a monist one; then we can further state that in so far as Alexander Dugin and the ENR identify with Guenon and Schuon and Lings and Nasr and all the other so-called "Traditionalists", that they are not traditional at all but have degenerated into a metaphysical (i.e. ontological and epistemological) outlook which is distinctly post-modern and hence anti-traditional. The perennialists have not comprehended the massive error of Kant's neumenon/ phenomenon distinction[6], and have thus fallen under its spell, just as they are spellbound by David Hume's numerous sleights of hand. One cannot claim to be either traditional or anti-modern or to be religious in any meaningful sense of the word if one does not have an objective epistemology. And again, we would even go as far as claiming that one cannot rationally assert a subjective epistemology, as such an assertion is self-undermining due to its internal logic which is infinitely regressive.

The post-moderns argue that "the narrating subject is never autonomous, never situated at an Archimedean point beyond space and time, never able to perceive the world with detachment and certainty."

---

6   The gentle reader is referred to the subsection entitled "The Rabbit Hole runs Deeper than Modernism and Kant's Copernican Revolution" in this volume; or better yet, to the *Pascedi* Encyclical itself.

14. Objective Truth and Radical Postmodern Subjectivism

(O'Meara). But precisely the opposite is true, as anything other than a foundational epistemology based on reason is self-undermining. The only way to stand on solid ground and orient oneself to a given direction and 'perceive the world with detachment and certainty' is by anchoring one's faculty of intellection by that special faculty of sapiential knowledge and wisdom we call revelation. Anything else will result in disorientation, angst, and nausea (roughly in that order).

The Perennialists claim to be saving religion from the onslaught of modernity, but by adopting a pluralist epistemology, and especially one that is applied to the truths at the core of a given religion, they are sacrificing its most essential element: sacrality; for if religion is deprived of its exclusive claim to absolute truth, then it is deprived of its sacrality and sacrosanctity and can no longer claim to be sacred. This, of course, is precisely the loss that the Perennialists claim to be avoiding. Ultimately, the whole movement is a modernist reaction which is supposedly against modernity. Again, you can't make this stuff up!

Extra Ecclesiam nulla Salus and its Alternative: the Zombification of the Soul

We started this section with a discussion of the logical and spiritual impossibility of the radical post-modern critique and its pluralist aftermath in the hopes of convincing our friends that the postmodern critique can serve a positive purpose if taken in small doses and not taken to excess. Postmodernism dismisses *all* truth and ethical values as nothing more than conventional social constructs, and this is akin to a scorched-earth policy which is a military strategy that aims to destroy anything that might be useful to the enemy while it is advancing through or withdrawing from a given location. It is not necessary to burn your own house down to the ground. There may be problems with Christianity, and there certainly are, but its basic moral teachings are fine. Its teachings on usury, first and foremost; its teachings on marriage and homosexuality; on euthanasia and suicide; on the primacy of the family unit; on differentiating the roles and identities of man and wife; on the Seven Deadly Sins, and so on and so forth – all of these are or should be self-evident. These are absolutely true, and if any culture does not abide by them, then that culture is the poorer for it. And it is not "racism" to say so. One should not try to impose one's culture on another's by force, even if that culture is inferior to one's own. This can and should only be done with the ineluctable persuasion which comes with loving kindness and a superior intellectual worldview and a superior spiritual station. But this indispensable imperative does not mean that "the differences between societies in any sense, can in no shape or form, imply the superiority of one over the other". Not at all, Brother Alexander. If we maintain the position that nothing is better or worse than anything else, and we deny the possibility of criticizing others because nothing is "objectively better [or worse] than the others", be they in our own culture or in that of another – it makes no difference – then we have *denied the possibility of good and evil*, and have therefore denied the possibility and need to distinguish and choose between them. This is the equivalent of being a no-show at the divine test that God has put before us. And this not only earns a failure grade, but is a turning up of one's nose to God's moral schema, as a refusal to participate in it is a tacit rejection of His plan and of His providence, which demands that we participate in a moral way of life whose criteria are communally maintained and enforced.

The soul is a faculty that enables its possessor to distinguish between right and wrong. In other words, one who cannot distinguish between right and wrong is, in some very important sense, no longer in possession of his or her soul. Moral relativists, then, are soulless creatures. They are moral zombies (their souls have shriveled and died). And what we would say is that those who claim that moral ambiguity obtains "absolutely" (in *that*, apparently, there is *no* ambiguity whatsoever…) are also devoid of souls, because there has to be an eschaton at the end of time to judge between these decisions in order to make them *actually* moral (i.e. everlasting and not temporary) and no longer moral *in potentia*; and if one has refused to partake in this decision-making process which obtains communally, then he or she will not be judged. Choosing not to decide is the choice that the angels will record in your Book of Deeds, and that is not a good choice; it is a failing grade that will ensure that your Book of Deeds will be given to you "behind your back" i.e. in ignominy, on Judgment Day, as the Quran tells us.

And we will go further than that and state to those who object that Islam is just another form of Judaism with all its arcane laws that were supposedly issued by some god, that the sacred eternal laws that are applicable universally and which issue forth by way of revelation are

14. Objective Truth and Radical Postmodern Subjectivism

also a necessary part of this moral choice. If one does not have a clear set of laws and a clear way of life that one is expected to follow, then one cannot reasonably be held accountable for anything on Judgment Day. If God's will (i.e. that which is right) is not *clear and universally applicable*, then arbitrary (individual) acts are just as valid as any other. And of course this is what Protestantism has slouched down to. And this makes a mockery of Judgment Day, as well as of Heaven and of Hell. Am I making myself clear? That is why Moslems believe that orthodox monotheism must necessarily include attaining to faith in the *exclusivity* of God's Providential Lordship (and submitting to it), *in addition to* belief in His being the sole creator – in the unicity of His creatorship.

There has to be a *clearly defined moral consensus-reality* against which one's soul is to be judged, and the failure of this to obtain or positively to affirm this tenet blows the whole popsicle stand out of the water. The absence of a clearly defined magisterium is what leads to nihilism. This is what moral pluralism comes down to: Scripture: *nihil*. Magisterium: *nihil*. Community consensus: *nihil*. Absolute basis of commonly-held morality: *nihil*. Confusion and lack of clarity, *a la* the demi-urge crypt: *copia et profusion*. Day of Judgement: *nihil*. Heaven and Hell: *inevitabili nihil*. Thus the soul also ineluctably turns into nothing, to *nihil*, because the soul depends on *all* of these elements which are its *hojjatic infrastructural prerequisites* without which it cannot function; it cannot exist *ex nihilo*, which is what the subjectivist and particularist epistemology of late modernity and postmodernity relegates it to, as does the cultural pluralism of the Perennialists, of the Grecists, and of Brother Alexander's Fourth Political Theory.

The need to conform one's way of life to this *clearly defined moral consensus-reality* is what religion has been traditionally defined as. A reality which is clearly defined, which provides a normative or moral framework on how one is to live one's life (complete with sacred ordinances, tenets and values), and upon which there is sacred consensus. This is the meaning of *extra Ecclesiam nulla salus* (outside the Church there is no salvation). There has to be an unimpeachable authority *(hojjat)*, to provide a paradigmatic example for the community to follow and to provide the perfect evidence of all truth (for those who did follow that example) and the conclusive argument and evidentiary proof against all falsehood (for those who did not follow that example) on Judgement Day. In the case of Shi'a Islam, this unimpeachable authority is the Imam of the Age, and in the Catholic tradition it is the institution and magisterium of the Church itself, which is an embodiment of God's sufficient télosic and testamentary proof against each person precluding any claims to ignorance in their trial on Judgment Day. In other words, there is a duty of care incumbent on God, on His Prophet, and on those who continue the sacred ministry of His Prophet, to provide an unimpeachable authority (*hojjat*) to the community of the faithful, and it is only when that unimpeachable authority is provided to the souls who are to be brought in front of their Maker for judgment, and if and only if these souls fail to make the right moral decisions in accordance with the criteria provided by this exemplary model and paradigmatic example, that there can be an argument made in the case that is being prepared against them on the Day of Judgement. Thus, it is obvious that an objective and *clearly defined moral consensus-reality* is necessary for souls to be able to make moral decisions and hence to be able to participate in the acid test which will allow them to pass the test and to be granted ever-lasting Heaven as a reward. The duty of care must be executed (*e'temām-e hojjat*). But pluralism, moral relativism and subjectivism all preclude such a consensus reality from obtaining, thus preventing the duty of care from being executed. They therefore engender and foster nihilism in the extreme by denying the soul its chance at a Final Judgement which can only obtain in the religions of the Abrahamic faiths on the basis of a *clearly defined* communal *moral consensus-reality*, because otherwise, the question becomes: How can one avoid nihilism if one holds that such a sacred consensus is *not* necessary for the progress of the soul from the earthly abode through to the Day of Judgment? If there is no criterion (*forqān*), how is one to be judged? How is one's fate to be determined come the Day of Reckoning? Is such judgment even conceivable without a touchstone that is recognized by the whole of the community? If so, how?

So much for Soren Kierkegaard's radical individual, whose soul he has sent to its perdition (by his denial of the *extra Ecclesiam nulla salus* dogma), where the real fear and trembling will no doubt begin.

Kierkegaard and other Protestants who follow his anti-establishmentarian teachings bring on damnation for themselves because they fail to realize the vital significance of the role the

14. Objective Truth and Radical Postmodern Subjectivism

Church plays in the salvation dramaturgy and in what we would call providing an unimpeachable authority (*hojjat*) in order to ensure that the duty of care is properly provided and executed (*e'temām-e hojjat*), so that the Court on the Day of Judgment can have legitimate legal standing. And that is why we caution our brothers in the Eurasianist Movement and in the European New Right, not just against subjectivist epistemologies and pluralist and particularist ontologies which do not have universal efficacy, but against positing any alternative system which is incomplete in so far as there is insufficient authority in it to allow the Court on the Day of Judgment to convene without sufficient legitimate legal standing. For by advocating any system that falls short of this vital criterion, you are participating in a zombification process and relegating yourselves and your followers and brothers in arms to their everlasting perdition. *Wa Allāhu ya'lam.*

(And of course if you readily admit that you do not believe in a Hereafter or a Day of Judgment, then you are admitting to holding a worldview that is already pessimistic and nihilistic in the extreme compared to Islam and traditional Christianity in that it sees man's life as being limited to the handful of years of the life of this material world, and denies man the possibility of everlasting bliss. And you will have betted on the wrong side of Pascal's Wager.)

And not to belabor the point but just to make sure that our interlocutors are following us on this. Call me Ishmael, but the Eurasianists and the Grecists tell us that they are against modernity and against its unrelenting onslaught on tradition; but perhaps they do not realize the implications of the subjectivist and anti-foundational epistemology and the particularist and pluralist and anti-universalist ontology which they believe in? Because we hope it is by now clear that such cultural pluralism and relativism denies the very possibility of *everything* that the traditional world stands for.

15. *Welāyat* and the Principal of *Tavallī* and *Tabarrī*

(Spiritual Affinity and the Principle of Avowal and Disavowal)

So we are coming to the end of our little essay, where we have endeavored to demonstrate by way of providing positive ideas and an alternative ideological model from the beliefs of the faith of Shi'a Islam to contrast with the ideas which we find to be wanting in the ideologies of Brother Alexander, Magister Michael Jones, Comrade Alain de Benoist and our friends in the European New Right. One of the most important tenets which we have tried to establish is that there is no getting away from having to lay down a corner stone and to build a solid foundation from solid first principles. But we want to go beyond that now, and to talk a little bit about what needs to happen (at least within our own tradition of Shi'a Islam) once those creedal foundations are laid and once faith in them is attained.

As stated above, moral relativists become moral zombies by virtue of the fact that they are no longer able to distinguish between right and wrong and to make moral choices. Those we will leave by the wayside, so that they can perchance get a walk on part in a John Carpenter film. And so we will move on to those who not only are still in possession of their souls but have the ontic capacity (*qābelīa*) of being conscious of God and of accepting the message of His Apostle, and to those who self-surrender their will to that of God's by entering into Islam, thus forming a community which is intent on living in accordance with God's will.

The issue of submitting one's will to that of God's and living in accordance with it, and of there *being* a will to submit to is a major subject that has been dealt with elsewhere.[1] And so we will have to content ourselves here by simply quoting an excerpt from one of Imam Ali's sermons on the subject of God's Will and Providential Lordship.

---

[1] Those who are interested to learn more about this key concept are referred to *The Exclusivity of Providential Lordship: Its Rational and Scriptural Proofs*, Lion of Najaf Publishers, 2017; or to the larger work, *Creedal Foundations of Walīyic Islam*.

The European New Right - A Shia Response

[What?!] Did God reveal a religion [to mankind] that is imperfect and [then] asked [man] for help in its completion? Are [we to suppose that] they are partners with God such that they can determine [for themselves] whatsoever they desire [of the laws of religion] and [expect] God to be pleased with this?? [Or] did God the Sublimely Exalted reveal a perfect religion, but that it was the Most Noble Prophet who failed properly to promulgate it? Whereas God the Sublimely Exalted stated, [6:38] *Not a single thing have We neglected in the Book.*

The implication that is clear to all but the postmoderns is that it makes no sense for the God who was so very exacting in His act of creation not to provide a perfect religion for the highest lifeform within His creation. We shall also provide an extended excerpt from the great German Roman Catholic ethicist and economist Heinrich Pesch who as the gentle reader will see, is fully cognizant of this perfection.

If an infinitely wise God is the creator of the world and the author of human nature, then He must have endowed His work with a purpose in conformity with His wisdom. *And he must also have established for his creatures with their various rankings a law suited to their nature, by which they are equipped with a rule for their existence and activity in accord with their natural purposes...* It would in fact be impossible for an all-wise God to operate without a plan and to submit the created world to total anarchy. That plan is not merely known by God, but it is also willed by the highest Lawgiver insofar as a law, a *lex aeterna*, existed eternally in him; and it emerged in the temporal world just as the world itself arose in time. In irrational creatures this law emerges as the principle and norm of their movement and activity, as a natural law or instinct. In rational man, in accordance with his nature, it emerges as the natural light of reason by which he recognizes what we must do and ought not to do, as the Divine moral law [the supra-natural light of revelation] which is destined to lead us to the goal intended by God in the way intended by Him.[2]

Thus, there is "a Divine moral law suited to [our] nature", a *lex aeterna*. And the community that attains to faith and is intent on living life in

---

2   Heinrich Pesch, *Lehrbuch der National Oekonomie*, Vol. I, Bk. 1, p. 138

15. Welāyat and the Principal of Tavallī and Tabarrī

accordance with this sacred eternal law and with the faith's precepts and ordinances and values is *purposive* as all of its members share the same goal. It is also *télosic* because they participate in a goal-oriented process whose end they all share in common, which is to attain to human perfection, to gain sapiential knowledge (*ma'refat*), to order society in a way that is in accord with God's justice and will, to draw near to Allāh (*qurb ilā allāh*), and ultimately, to encounter the Countenance of God (*liqā'ollāh*).

Those who have the ontic capacity (*qābelīa'*) of being conscious of God and of accepting the message of His Apostle, and who self-surrender their will to that of God's by entering into Islam, form a community which is intent on living in accordance with God's will. This unity of purpose engenders a *spiritual affinity* between the members of the community in the sense that *they are proximate to each other in the order of creation and proximate to the Imams and to the Prophet, and therefore, by extension, to God Himself* (relative to the rest of humanity and to the other orders of being within creation). This spiritual proximity and affinity is referred to in the Shi'a literature as *welāya^t*. When the word *welāya^t* is used generally, it means closeness, proximity, connectedness, contiguity, affinity, and can even cover the wider semantic field that encompasses the predilection, harmony, and spiritual and creedal kinship between two or more people or things. When two things are inter-related and inter-twined in such a way that it is not possible to separate them, it is said that they have *welāya^t*. When we say that you and I have welāya^t, what is meant here is that we are closely connected to each other, we have a close affinity and a mutual dependence on one another. Thus, welāya^t means the bond between two things or persons.

To the above definition, we can add that *welāya^t* is a multifaceted term which ultimately defies translation; its range of meaning includes, at a minimum, the following different facets which we have been able to glean from the literature: 1. Closeness or proximity, 2. contiguity, 3. affinity, 4. cohesion, 5. friendship, 6. dominion, 7. sovereignty, 8. proxy sovereignty or regency, 9. guardianship, 10. governance, 11. jurisdiction, 12. reign, 13. Command, and 14. custodianship. *Welāya^t* means spiritual proximity to God but in most Shi'a contexts also refers to the regency or guardianship-type sovereign authority which is vested in the Fourteen Immaculates as a result of that proximity.

The European New Right - A Shia Response

Welāyat refers to a special type of *sovereignty* that is the central pillar of the Shi'a conception of the imāmate or the Islamic vision of the way in which the polity of the community is to be structured, with the imām or leader of the community having walīyic or guardianship-type sovereignty over his adherents, and to whom a pledge of allegiance is due, which affirms the Imams' regency over the affairs of the community.[3]

So to step back again, what is important to note is that when there is a *lex aeterna* or sacred law (*sharī'a*) which is the criterion for distinguishing between right and wrong, and which therefore functions in the capacity of enabling the soul to make moral decisions (and therefore to attain to eternal Heaven thereby; providing the ground and possibility for living a moral life, a Final Judgment, and its ever-lasting reward), then this moral reality, which is at the same time a metaphysical reality, means that right and wrong obtain metaphysically and absolutely, and that there is a right way and a wrong way of doing things and of living one's life; and subsequently, that those whose lives and spirits are most closely conformed to this reality and will of God have the greatest affinity (*welāyat*) to God's will and Providential Lordship (*rububīat*), and those whose spirits have slightly less affinity are a degree removed, and so on down a pyramidal hierarchy of spiritual kinship and proximity (*welāyat*) to God. The spiritual and moral character of the prophets and Imams is such that God has chosen them to be His representatives on Earth (*khalīfat ol'lāh fī'l ard*), which is why the members of the community that attains to faith in and is intent on living life in accordance with the precepts and ordinances and values of this sacred eternal law and integral (or "totalitarian" if you prefer) moral system gains spiritual proximity to God thereby. And this is why the nature of the Shi'a moral vision or the way in which the polity of the community is to be structured is one where the imām or leader of the community must

---

3   According to Shi'a belief, the sovereign authority which is vested in the Fourteen Immaculates as a result of their proximity to God is vested (by way of scriptural as well as rational proofs) in feqhicity in the Era of the Occultation (i.e. in the era of the absence of the Imam of the Age from the physical plane); where feqhicity (feqāhat) or the Shi'a magisterium refers to the body of authoritative ethico-legal and doctrinal religious teachings for which there is consensus or near-consensus within Shi'a Islam, together with the body of the Shi'a clerisy who have the authority (based on their knowledge and learning) to expound upon and elucidate these religious truths.

15. Welāyat and the Principal of Tavallī and Tabarrī

necessarily have *walīyic* or guardianship-type sovereignty over his adherents, i.e. it is due to his *walīyic* station, or to the proximity of his spiritual station to God, and consequently, to the affinity of the office of his guardianship-type sovereignty (*welāya'*) to that of God's will. (Additionally, because God bestows the angel of immaculacy (*esma'*) upon the prophets and the Imams, their investiture in the office of guardianship-type sovereignty (*welāya'*) is sinless and inerrant.) With giving a pledge of allegiance (*bay'a'*) to the *walīy* or the leader (imām) who has guardianship-type sovereignty over the community of those who have attained to faith, the true believers (*al-mo'minīn*) enter into a covenantal commitment to the Exclusivity of God's Providential Lordship (*towhīd-e rububīa'*) by way of God's true representative on Earth (*khalīfa' ol'lāh fī'l ard*) (as opposed to living their lives under the auspices of those who have illegitimately usurped and profaned this sacred office). Thus, welayat being a spiritual station of proximity to the source of all reality and being, can also be said to include a major facet which can be translated as spiritual gravity or ontic amplitude.

Thus we can now say that one of the primary differences between Western and Islamic civilization lies hidden in this essential and fundamental religious tenet of fidelity (*towhīd*) and infidelity (*sherk*) to the covenantal commitment to the Exclusivity of God's Providential Lordship over the Social Order of His Creation. Modern civilization released its grip from God's hand, i.e. revealed guidance, and replaced it with its own self-proclaimed system of the overstretched jurisdiction and compass of reason applied only to the observable world to the exclusion of the much greater world that is beyond the ken of ordinary perception (*ālam al-ghayb*), in order to be able "better" to understand man and the environment in which he finds himself, and in order to be able to change it. And while it is true that, at least in its initial phases, modern man could indeed still attain to faith in God and would at times even strive to prove His existence, but even so, the province of the activity of his God was limited to the confines of the four walls of his churches and no longer had any social efficacy or compass, and was absent, vacant, occulted, when it came to the community's political economy and to the culture at large.

The bond of *welāyat* which we discussed above is the umbilicus that nurtures and sustains the community of the Devotees of God – which modern man severed with the advent of the Age of Reason

The European New Right - A Shia Response

(or the Second Reformation which followed the original one). This bond is formed and sustained on the basis of attaining to faith in the essential and fundamental religious tenet of fidelity (*towhīd*) and infidelity (*sherk*) to the covenantal commitment to the Exclusivity of God's Providential Lordship over the Social Order of His Creation. Its concomitant tenet is the all-important and logically necessary principle of *tawallī* and *tabarrī: tawallī* (affinity; camaraderie; friendship; community – it is derived from the same root as *walīy* and *welāya*) toward those who have attained to faith in *towhīd* and are true to the covenant they made with their *rabb* (Lord of Providence, Manager, Nurturer, and Sustainer) on the Day of Alast[4], and *berā'at* or *tabarrī* (disavowal; execration; anathematization) towards those who have failed to attain to faith in *towhīd* and have thus broken their covenant. We say that it is a logically necessary principle because in any system that is purposive, there is movement; and that movement is directed *toward* a goal and *away from* its opposite. Or as my friend Michael Jones would put it, towards *logos* and away from *anti-logos*. And needless to say, all moral systems are purposive, and therefore necessarily exclusionary. And not to belabor the point, but when Brother Alexander states that "Eurasianism, recognizing the pretense of the Western logos to universality, refuses to recognize this universality" he is rightly engaged in a righteous act of moral exclusion against a hegemonic force which has no right to universal implementation but wants to achieve "full spectrum domination" regardless. We are with Brother Alexander, and proclaim with him unashamedly: to Hell with them! But equally, he is wrong when he says that

> "Societies can be compared, but we cannot state that any one of them is objectively better than the others. Such an assessment is always subjective, and any attempt to raise a subjective assessment to the status of a theory is racism. This type of an attempt is unscientific and inhumane. The differences between

---

4 See the commentaries associated with the following āya: [7:172] And whenever thy Rabb (Lord of Providence, Manager, Nurturer, and Sustainer) brings forth their offspring from the loins of the children of Adam, He [thus] calls upon them to bear witness about themselves: "Am I not your Rabb?" – to which they answer: "Yea, indeed, we do bear witness thereto!" [Of this We remind you,] lest you say on the Day of Resurrection, "Verily, we were unaware of this". See for example *Creedal Foundations of Walīyic Islam* for a full treatment of the subject and the implications of this azalic covenant to the form that the Islamic polity must necessarily take presented from an emic Shi'a perspective.

15. Welāyat and the Principal of Tavallī and Tabarrī

societies in any sense can, in no shape or form, imply the superiority of one over the other."

Rather, it is not a simple question of whether it is an objective or subjective position. From our (emic) point of view, our position is grounded in a reality whose certainty is as solid as bedrock, but from an etic point of view, our reality may not be objective, but neither is it subjective; rather, it is inter-subjective; that is, it is a reality that we all share as members who have attained to faith in a given creed or set of first principles which make up our collective and purposive constitutional order. And this is not "racism" or ethno-centrism or nationalism, but religio-centrism, which requires righteous acts of moral exclusion against any and all who oppose the moral universe of which we are certain. It is the principle of *tawallī* and *tabarrī*, which is a necessary part of our creed. The difference is that unlike the barbarians who want to impose their "liberal" order on us by economic coercion (and when that fails, by military force),[5] it is not incumbent on us to impose our beliefs on others, merely to inform others that this other possibility exists.

وَإِن تُطِيعُوهُ تَهْتَدُوا ۚ وَمَا عَلَى الرَّسُولِ إِلَّا الْبَلَاغُ الْمُبِينُ

[24:54] If you obey the Apostle, you will be rightly guided, for the Apostle is not bound to do more than deliver the clear message [entrusted to him].

The Quran tells the Prophet, and by implication, the community of those who have attained to faith in God's message for which the Prophet acted as a channel, to use reasoned argumentation in dealing with the unbelievers. The Quran itself is scripture, but it is full of rational proofs which have been revealed to aid in this very purpose. But when reason does not succeed, as it inevitably will not with some, the rationale of the following *sūra* (division) becomes operative:

[109:1] Say: "O you who refuse to believe in the truth!

[109:2] "I do not worship that which you worship,

---

5   I am reminded of the late William F. Buckley who famously said that Liberals claim to want to give a hearing to other views, but then are shocked and offended to discover that there are other views.

[109:3] "and neither do you worship Him Whom I worship!

[109:4] "and [what is more,] I will not worship that which you have [ever] worshipped,

[109:5] nor will you [ever] worship Him Whom I worship.

[109:6] "[Therefore,] unto you be your way, and unto me, mine!"

We live in a part of the world where not too long ago, our barbarian neighbors Dāesh (or ISIS) were within forty kilometers of our western border and wanted nothing more than to be able to breach it and cut all our heads off. In such a situation, can one seriously maintain that "Societies can be compared, but we cannot state that any one of them is objectively better than the others"? It is obvious to me that Brother Alexander does not really believe that. For if he did, why would he be the greatest advocate of the necessity of the Russian Federation's sending troops to Syria to kill off these vermin? We want to engage the Wahhabeasts in debate (their so-called "scholars"), but they refuse, preferring instead to cut off our heads. It is ridiculous to maintain in this case that the Iranian civilization is not superior to the one the takfiris are attempting to create; even a child will tell you which community is the superior one.

I have at times joked that "I am not anti-semitic, I'm anti-*Jewish*". But I hasten to add that my interlocutor should not be mistaken in that I am *only* anti-Jewish. That would truly be racist or bigoted or both. But I am also anti-Christian, anti-Hindu, anti-atheist, anti-agnostic, anti-sitting on the fence, and anti-any and all other religions and modalities of identity other than my own.[6] I can't help it! I am *against* any and all systems of thought, ideologies and ways of life that I am not *for*. Does that not make perfect sense? If it does (and it surely does), then it also follows that this whole modern fuss about the need to be politically correct and not to be against this and against that is perfect *non*sense. It is a simple matter of the definition of what being "for" something means, and the definition of what having any sort of identity or religion means. Thus, it is not just me that is anti-this and anti-that; anyone who has any sense of identity that has any sense of worth is at one and the same time against anything that is not part of that identity. It is a matter of simple logic (a logic that has been veiled by that perniciously

---

6   See āya 5:51, below.

15. Welāyat and the Principal of Tavallī and Tabarrī

deceptive latter day religion known as Liberalism, which on one hand is relativist in this sense, but is radically and viciously universalist in the other sense of its voracious appetite in wanting to impose itself on others). You, gentle reader, are just like me, unless your mind has been so corrupted by the toxicity of epistemological and cultural pluralism that it has degenerated into an amorphous blob and you have become so zombified as to no longer be able to differentiate between who you are and are not, let alone between right and wrong.

The problem, dear Alexander, dear Perennialists, dear cultural relativists, dear postmodernists, is not the assertion of a morally or intellectually superior position. If that were the case, I would have no justification in writing this essay and Brother Alexander could not justify writing all of his wonderful books, because the Forth Political Theory would not be advocating a position that is intellectually superior to the First, Second or Third. I have no problem whatsoever with Liberalism's assertion that their position is morally and intellectually superior to mine, nor even with the fact that they assert that it is universally superior to all other positions (that their superiority has universal applicability). I don't even have a problem with their wanting to impose their absurd system on me and on the rest of the world. How can I? That is exactly what I believe of *my* system and my point of view. And what is more, I have no *choice* in the matter. If I choose not to decide, I still have made a choice. Or as I have stated above (in the immediately previous section on Objective Truth), we are syntactically hard-wired to this ineluctability. Any negation of an absolutist position will necessarily either be absolutist itself or will be no negation at all: "All absolutist positions are [absolutely] wrong". Where the *real* problem lies is when the liberals or anyone else (including, not least, the absurdly mistaken Moslems[7] who fall into this trap) want to impose their system *by force*, rather than through peaceful and rational debate. In that, the militant liberals who feel the "responsibility to protect" everyone from a way of life that is at variance with their own are qualitatively no different than Dāesh, and quantitatively much worse, so much so that Dāesh is merely a tool in their nasty playbook.

---

[7] For the difference between Sunni and Shi'a sacred-juridical (feqhic) positions on the issue of preemptive warfare (jehād-e ebtedāī), see Dāvūd Feirahī's *War and Military Ethics in* Shi'a *Islam.*

The European New Right - A Shia Response

All right; so much for our rational arguments and proofs. Let us move to the scriptural ones. The following *āya* describes the bond that obtains between those who have attained to faith as arising from their emigrating from "the domain of evil" to create a new community of their own that is free of those old ungodly values:

> [8:72] Behold, as for those who have attained to faith, *and who have forsaken the domain of evil* and are striving hard, with their possessions and their lives, in God's cause, as well as those who shelter and succor [them] - these are [truly] the friends and protectors of one another.

Thus, the bond between the true believers obtains with emigration and not just with faith: faith alone is not enough; the old values must be disavowed. The bond of *welāyat*, which is a social and therefore political phenomenon, and which is a seminal event in the individual and communal lives of the faithful of the community, is realized by striving together in the way of God, by *disavowal of the values of the old order*, and by emigrating to new climes where the faithful can live close to each other and work together to achieve the same common purposes. This is the principle of *berā'at* or *tabarrī* (disavowal; execration; anathematization) and *tawallī* (affinity; camaraderie; friendship; community): disavowing the enemies of God and those who have rejected His Prophet and His guidance, and at one and the same time, showing special kindness and mercy towards those who submit to God's providential lordship, subscribe to its values and are thus a part of the community of faith.

This important creedal principle, is based on several Quranic āyas, the most important of which are the following:

> [9:1] Disavowal by God and His Apostle [is herewith announced] unto those who ascribe divinity to aught beside God, [and] with whom you [O: believers] have made a covenant.

> [5:51] O you who have attained to faith! Do not take the Jews and the Christians for your allies: they are but allies of one another and whoever of you allies himself with them becomes, verily, one of them; behold, God does not guide such evildoers.

> [48:29] Mohammad is God's Apostle; and those who are [truly]

15. Welāyat and the Principal of Tavallī and Tabarrī

with him are firm and unyielding towards all deniers of the truth, [yet] full of mercy towards one another.

These *āyas* and others like them command Moslems to make a distinction between those who have attained to faith in God and in His Prophet and submitted to his Law (i.e. become members of the community of Moslems), being "firm and unyielding towards all deniers of the truth, yet full of mercy towards one another." This is a creedal principle of the Moslem community of faith. Thus,

> [9:71] And [as for] the believers, both men and women, they are close unto one another.

While at the same time, we are told,

> [8:73] With all this, [remember that] those who are bent on denying the truth are allies of one another;

and:

> [45:19] …Verily, such evildoers are but friends and protectors of one another.

Thus the principle of *tabarrī* (disavowal; execration; anathematization) and *tawallī* (camaraderie; friendship; community): disavowing the enemies of God and those who have rejected His Prophet and His guidance, and at one and the same time, showing special kindness and mercy towards those who submit to God's providential lordship and are a part of the community of faith, is what brings about and strengthens spiritual proximity (*welāya'*) between the believers, thus bringing about the religious uniformity which enables them to coalesce in community rather than as the atomized individuals who form the constituents of what has come to be known as "civil society", but which is, for all intents and purposes, a form of community which has degenerated to the point that it is no longer in harmony with man's *fetra* (primordial disposition), and which thus alienates him from his true nature, and is no longer communal in any meaningful sense of the word.

Modern man replaced commitment to the divine will (and connectedness to the umbilicus of His Providential Lordship) in favor of commitment and connectedness to his lower urges and desires, having given reason an overplus of jurisdiction, whereby its scope infringed upon that which was rightly the domain of revelation. This is why the Moslem community disavows, execrates and anathematizes Western modernity and all of its ungodly values and objectives. The political theology of Islamic civilization revolves around fidelity to the covenantal acceptance of and commitment to the Exclusivity of God's Providential Lordship over the Social Order of His Creation (*towhīd*). *Towhīd* is usually translated as "monotheism", which, given the above elaboration of its true meaning, can now be seen to be an inadequate rendition of the concept and creedal tenet. The "monotheism" of Islamic civilization is an all-encompassing one which, like an omnipresent spirit, encompasses and infuses all of the domains of man's existence, from the individual and communal to the worldly and otherworldly: man's freedom and independence, his knowledge and power, and his social policies and objectives and judgements – all are *towhīdic* in the sense that they are based on the commitment to God's exclusivity of providential Lordship over His creation and are defined and sustained by this all-embracing basic principle and tenet of the faith which depends upon the principle of *tabarrī* and *tawallī* for its establishment and maintenance. And that is why we continue to say "Death to America", not because we are a superior civilization to that of Liberalism's, which we are, or that we want to impose ourselves over others by force, which we do not; but because force can only be met with force.

Summary and Conclusion

What conclusion can we possibly draw from all of what we have said? We tackled the methodological error of grafting Christianity onto philosophy, and then bemoaning modernity when the philosophical tradition which Christianity hitched its boat to took a turn for the worse and started eating its own tail. We tackled the methodological error of philosophy *per se*, which, having deprived itself of the light of revelation, has failed to come up with a single first principle that all or even a majority (or plurality!) of philosophers can agree with. We proved the existence of God through rational means, rejecting Kierkegaards "leap of faith" as being both irrational and unnecessary, and proved that reason itself sees its own limitations and shortcomings when it comes to all of the domains of creation, which includes "the domain which is beyond the ken of ordinary human perception" (*al-ghayb*), and thus bows to true revelation when it encounters it, recognizing that revelation speaks of a realm concerning which reason has no jurisdiction. We refuted Heideggerian subjectivism on the grounds that being is indeed time-bound, but that this is the being of our soul, and not of our spirit, whose destiny lies in a world that lies beyond the time-bound limits of this world, in the world of the hereafter which has an incomparably higher ontic amplitude and intensity than that of this, the lowest world and the lowest order of being. And finally we refuted subjectivism more generally and its corollary, cultural pluralism, on the grounds that such a position is logically untenable, and because it is nihilistic in the extreme, bringing about what we characterized as a "zombification" of the soul, on the grounds that the soul is that human faculty that enables its possessor to distinguish between right and wrong, and that one who cannot distinguish between right and wrong is, in some very important sense, no longer in possession of his or her soul, and is a "dead man walking".

Moral relativists, we said, are soulless creatures or zombies. We went on to say that there has to be a *clearly defined moral consensus-reality* against which one's soul is to be judged, because the soul depends on a normative or moral framework on how one is to live one's life (complete with sacred ordinances, tenets and values), upon which there is sacred consensus, in order for it to be able to make communally binding moral decisions; it depends on this *hojjatic* infrastructural prerequisite, without which it cannot function. We posited that this was the ultimate meaning of the Catholic dogma known as *extra Ecclesiam nulla salus* (outside the Church there is no salvation): that there has to be a divinely-sanctioned unimpeachable authority *(hojjat)*, to provide a paradigmatic example for the community to follow so that if they failed to follow this example, the case will have been made against them, and the Court of Judgement at the Resurrection will thus have standing and be able to make its argument. Thus, we argued, an *objective* reality, which also must necessarily include a *clearly defined moral consensus-reality* is necessary for souls to be able to make moral decisions and hence to be able to participate in the acid test which will allow them to pass the test and to be granted ever-lasting Heaven as a reward. This is part and parcel of the duty of care which must be properly exercised by God and His divine agents (*e'temām-e hojjat*). We then went on to say that because pluralism, moral relativism and subjectivism all preclude such a consensus reality from obtaining, they prevent this duty of care from being executed and therefore engender and foster nihilism in the extreme by denying the soul its chance at a Final Judgement which can only obtain on the basis of a *clearly defined* communal *moral consensus-reality.*

* * *

So given all this, what are the choices before us? Alexander Dugin states that "It is the dusk of logos, the end of order, the last chord of masculine, exclusivist domination" and that therefore, there are three choices that can be made concerning the future.

> The first possible solution is the return to the kingdom of logos, the Conservative Revolution, the restoration of male full-scale domination in all spheres of the life — in philosophy, religion, and in everyday life... It is an effort to save the falling logos, the restoration of traditional society, and the eternally new Order.

> The second possible solution is to accept the current trends and to follow the direction of confusion, becoming more and more involved in the dissipation of structure, in post-structuralism, and trying to get pleasure out of the comfortable glide into nothingness. That is the option chosen by the Left and the

Summary and Conclusion

liberal representatives of postmodernity. It is modern nihilism at its best. The construction of a rational realm... [and] the incalculable multitudes of the flowers of putrefaction.

A third path [would be to] try to transcend the borders of logos... Seen from the standpoint of logos in general, including its most decayed aspects, beyond the domain of order lies nothing. So crossing the border of being is ontologically impossible. So, no one can cross that frontier into the non-existent not-being that simply is not. [But] If we insist, nevertheless, in doing this, then we should appeal to chaos in its original Greek sense, as to something that proceeds being and order, something pre-ontological... Logos cannot save us from the situation that it is the cause of. Logos is of no use to us here anymore. Only the pre-ontological chaos can give as a hint about how to go beyond the trap of postmodernity.

We agree that the first two are no choices, but the third is no choice at all either, because it is not a choice so much as a desire to get away from where we are at in a vague direction that is indeterminate. It is an "anywhere but here" non-option. Here is Brother Alexander's own assessment of the situation:

The architecture of the postmodern world is completely fragmented, perverse and confused. It is a labyrinth without an exit, as folded and twisted as a Moebius strip. Logos, which was the guarantor of strictness and order, serves here instead to grant curvature and crookedness...

He then goes on to say that "Logos has expired and we all will be buried under its ruins unless we make an appeal to chaos ..." and that "Perhaps this is 'the other beginning' Heidegger spoke of. But in one of his last interviews[1] Heidegger declared:

"Philosophy will not be able to bring about a direct change of the present state of the world. This is true not only of philosophy but of all merely human meditations and endeavors. Only a god can still save us."[2]

---

1   *Der Spiegel* Interview with Rudolf Augstein and Georg Wolff, carried out on 23 September 1966, which had been forbidden for publication before Heidegger's death in May 1976. It was published in May 31, 1976.

2   The rest of his train of thought for the curious is as follows (but to our mind, the statement

The European New Right - A Shia Response

Like William Golding, Heidegger makes the right diagnosis, but, again like William Golding who believed that "no ship was coming to save the ship-wrecked children", errs concerning the coming of the Universal Savior. Well, we will have to agree to disagree concerning that issue, but it would seem that we all agree, atheists or not, on the *need* for divine intervention. And so, in a sense, the conclusion is a simple one. As Yogi Berra once famously said, If you see a fork in the road, take it.

But being a Shi'a Moslem, I consider it my duty to end with words of warning which are taken from the Quran, which we believe is a collection of the exact words of God, as channeled by the Prophet Mohammad over a period of twenty-three years in seventh century Mecca and Medina. All these centuries ago God asked us a question that resonates strongly with us still today:

> [57:16] Has not the time arrived for the hearts of all who have attained to faith to feel humbled at the remembrance of God and of all the truth that has been bestowed [on them] from on high, lest they become like those who were granted revelation aforetime, and whose hearts have hardened with the passing of time so that many of them are [now] depraved?

But then God warns us that indeed people will not take heed, until it is too late. Until a terrible event will "make the skies bring forth a pall of smoke enveloping the people" – a nuclear war, perhaps, bringing on nuclear winter. And then He tells us that the people who turned their back on the message of the Prophet of Islam and who didn't take anything seriously in their heedlessness and skepticism, will suffer a grievous chastisement and will beg for relief, but that it will be too late for them.

> [44:9] Nay, but they [who lack inner certainty] take nothing seriously, amusing themselves [in their state of uncertainty]. [44:10] *Await, then, for the Day when the skies shall bring forth a pall of smoke which will make obvious [the approach of the*

---

is best left truncated): "I think the only possibility of salvation left to us is to prepare readiness, through thinking and poetry, for the appearance of the god or for the absence of the god during the decline; so that we do not, simply put, die meaningless deaths, but that when we decline, we decline in the face of the absent god."

Summary and Conclusion

Last Hour], [at which event your uncertainty will vanish] [44:11] enveloping the people, [and causing the sinners to exclaim:] "Grievous is this suffering! [44:12] [Having been awakened from their state of heedlessness by this torment, the unbelievers will say,] "O our Lord and Sustainer, relieve us of this suffering, for, verily, we [now] believe [in Thee]!" [44:13] [But] how shall this [tardy] awakening avail them [at the Last Hour], seeing that an apostle had already come unto them previously, clearly expounding the truth, [44:14] whereupon they turned their backs on him and accused him of being tutored by men [and not inspired by Heaven as he claimed, and that they accused him of being] a madman [for wanting to pull off such a supposed deception].

And Allāh knows best.

* * *

Praise be to Allāh, the Lord of the Two Worlds, for enabling us to bring this essay to a close. We are responsible for the shortcomings within it; and to Allāh is due the credit and praise for any good that might come from it.

www.ingramcontent.com/pod-product-compliance
Lightning Source LLC
Chambersburg PA
CBHW060822190426
43197CB00038B/2194